PROPHECIES
CONCEALED
NOW
REVEALED

PROPHECIES CONCEALED NOW REVEALED
Published by: Voice of Evangelism Outreach Ministries
P. O. Box 3595
Cleveland, TN 37320
www.voe.org
423.478.3456

ISBN: 978-0-9785920-8-0
Copyright © 2016 by Perry F. Stone, Jr.
First edition printed 2016
Printed in the United States of America

Cover Design/Layout: Michael Dutton

Discover *a* Biblical Breakthrough *that* Solves *the* Mystery
of the Pre-Tribulation Rapture

PERRY SIUNE

PROPHECIES

CONCEALED
NOW
REVEALED

GOD'S FUTURE PROPHETIC CALENDAR:
*The Rapture, Tribulation & Thousand Year Reign of Christ
are concealed in Israel's Three Remaining Fall Festivals!*

CONTENTS

CHAPTER 1

End Time Parallels of the Days of Lot and Noah

"There were giants in the earth in those days;
and also after that, when the sons of God
came in unto the daughters of men, and they
bear children to them, the same became mighty
men which were of old, men of renown."

– GENESIS 6:4 (KJV)

O NE OF THE greatest mysteries in Scripture is the Genesis narrative that reveals a race of superhuman men called giants that once roamed the planet. There is consensus among numerous scholars that these giants were the offspring of fallen angels who took upon themselves the form of men and lusted after the beautiful women. They engaged in sexual activity and procreated a strange breed of beings on Earth that were considered demi-gods—part human and part "divine." These "sons of God" were angels sent to Earth to teach men to follow the Lord, but they became enslaved by the sinful atmosphere sometime after they were sent to Earth.

One of two words translated as giants in Genesis 6:4 is *nephilim*, from the root *naphal*, meaning *to fall*. Perhaps this refers to the fall of the angels responsible for their birth. The New Testament tells us that these fallen angels are now bound in the lower compartment of hell

(KJV), which in the Greek is Tartarus—the lowest hell—where they await the final judgment (see 2 Peter 2:4 and Jude 6).

Notice a prophetic parallel. There were *fallen ones* on the earth prior to Noah's flood; and Paul wrote that, prior to the return of Christ, a *falling away* (defection from truth) will occur before the man of sin, the Antichrist, is revealed (2 Thess. 2:3). As in the days of Noah, at the time of the end, the *fallen ones* will be a central feature as people defect from the truth. The last event the flood generation saw was water sweeping the earth. Daniel wrote that, when the Antichrist assumes control, the end will be with a flood (Dan. 9:26). This refers to unceasing wars and desolation that will span the entire world, all at once.

MODIFICATION OF HUMANS

When counting from the creation of Adam to the approximate year of the flood, we come to the year 1,656. Moses wrote that there were ten generations of men from Adam to Noah, and recorded the age of each man when his first son was born.

Here are the ages of the fathers when their first sons were born:

- Seth was 105

- Enos was 90

- Cainan was 70

- Mahalalel was 65

- Jared was 160

- Enoch was 65

- Methesulah was 187

- Lamech was 182

- Noah was 500

We are uncertain how many children were in each individual family, but we know men lived much longer. The longest living pre-flood man, Methuselah, died in his 969th year (Gen. 5:27). Some scholars and researchers have attempted to estimate the possible number of people that lived on the earth the moment the flood erupted. It is suggested that, if each man had an average of six children, with the lifespan at that time, there could have been as many as 235 million individuals living on the earth.

The one unanswerable question is this: how many giants were living on the earth before the flood? Throughout the years, especially in the 1800s, newspapers around the world carried reports that bones of giants were found in caves, excavations, Indian tombs, and so forth. There is evidence that, in the early days of man, giants were scattered around the world. There may have been tens of thousands of giants by the time God executed the flood judgment. God took notice of the world's corrupt condition, as the Genesis text indicates:

> "And God saw the wickedness of man was great in the earth, and that every imagination of the thoughts of his heart was only evil continually."
>
> – GEN. 6:5 (KJV)

The word imagination in Hebrew is *yetser* and refers to a form, but figuratively can allude to conception. This idea of the "conception" in his heart being evil continually can mean that seed thoughts and imaginations were evil; but it can also be a clue that men were caught up in this man-giant conception sweeping the world. This procreative manipulation not only affected humans, but a careful study of specific phrases in Genesis 6 indicates that some form of manipulation also involved animals. God warned that He would destroy both man and beast, because *"I am sorry that I have made them"* (Gen. 6:7). It is likely that the sexual perversion had spread to bestiality, an abominable sin that led to the death penalty under the Law of God (Lev. 20:15). Another verse that exposed this corruption of the animal kingdom is Genesis 6:12: "God looked upon the earth and indeed it was corrupt; for all flesh had corrupted their way upon the earth." Notice both men and beast–all flesh—was corrupt, or in a decaying process (especially in a moral sense).

While the Genesis account does not elaborate on this corrupted flesh, it is mentioned in the book of Jasher—a book referred to twice in the Bible (Josh. 10:13; 2 Sam. 1:18). A copy of the book of Jasher was discovered and translated in 1840. The writer, commenting on the flood narrative, gave a hint of the manipulation involving animals:

> "And the sons of men in those days took from the cattle of the earth, the beasts of the field and the fowls of the air, and taught the mixture of animals of one species with the other, in order wherewith to provoke the Lord; and the Lord saw that the whole earth was corrupt, for all flesh had corrupted its ways upon earth, all men and all animals."
>
> – JASHER 4:18

In this narrative, we see a prophetic parallel with today's genetic manipulation of DNA. Researchers have used the DNA of both animals and humans as they attempt to clone an exact replica of animals or humans. Scientists have cloned lambs, and have been experimenting with human DNA in their efforts to clone a child with a specific eye color, hair color, and gender. They suggest that eventually, parents will have the ability to choose the physical appearance of their child through DNA manipulation and genetic modification. Many researchers consider this a great scientific breakthrough. However, it appears to others that humans are attempting to take the place of God.

There is neither biblical or sacred religious history to prove the following, but some biblical researchers believe that undocumented mingling of the seeds led to strange creatures being birthed that had both human and animal features. They suggest that some of the early signs in the heaven, as well as Greek and other mythologies, are based upon these genetic mixtures that were part human and part animal. We do not know for certain how the odd images of ancient false gods and goddesses originated; but we do know that giants were the central cause of the flood. Had God permitted the fallen angels to continue their perversion without wiping out most of the human race, all flesh would have been perverted and the world as we know it would not exist.

NOAH—THE UNTAINTED DNA

All flesh was corrupt, except that of Noah. His great-grandfather Methuselah was another righteous man who was living right before the flood. What significant factors marked Noah? First, Noah found grace in the eyes of the Lord (Gen. 6:8). The Hebrew word grace is *chen,* spelled with two Hebrew letters, chet and nun. The name Noah is *Noach* in Hebrew, spelled with these same two letters reversed: nun and chet. The name Noah means *rest.* Noah was a "just man," (Gen. 6:9), the word *just* being the Hebrew word *tsaddiq,* meaning blameless and righteous before God. Noah was "perfect in his generations" (Gen. 6:9). The word *perfect* refers to being complete and without blemish. However, in this context, it emphasizes that Noah was *undefiled* by the corruption surrounding him.

This idea of Noah being uncorrupted has much deeper meaning than uncompromising righteousness. The fallen angels, giants, and their offspring had corrupted the *blood line* of humanity. Not only were their imaginations evil continually, but every person on Earth, in some form, was being perverted, corrupted, and defiled by the wickedness of fallen angels and giants—offspring that God predicted would be the "seed of Satan" (see Gen. 3:15). The Cain linage was part of the seed of Satan, while Noah emerged from the Seth linage. Being "perfect" indicated that Noah's bloodline, going back to Adam, had not been corrupted by the DNA, or seeds, of the giants. Imagine God looking over the entire Earth and finding only one man who could be selected to save his family from destruction.

THE ORIGIN OF IDOLS

When did idolatry begin? There is no record of idols prior to the flood. The first warning against worshipping false gods was given to Israel after they departed Egypt. History indicates the Egyptians worshipped numerous gods, along with the Babylonians and later the Greeks and Romans.

While this explanation of the origin of idolatry may seem too simplistic, there is a belief that the giants and their children, both before and after the flood, became legends (men of renown, see Gen. 6:4). Several early church fathers indicated that both the giants and their children were given names, and centuries later were worshipped as gods. Justin Martyr (100–165 AD) wrote:

> "[God] committed the care of men and all things under heaven to angels whom he appointed over them. But the angels transgressed this appointment, and were captivated by the love of women, and begot children who were those that are called demons; and besides, they afterwards subdued the human race to themselves, partly by teaching them to offer sacrifices, and incense and libations, of which they stood in need after they were enslaved by lustful passions; and among them they sowed murders, wars, adulteries, intemperate deeds, and all wickedness.
>
> Whence also the poets and mythologists, not knowing that it was the angels and those demons whom had been begotten by them did these things to men, and women, and cities, and nations which they related, ascribed them to god himself, and to the offspring of those who were called brothers, Neptune and Pluto, and to the children again of these their offspring.
>
> For whatever name each of the angels had given himself and his children, by that name they were called them."
>
> – JUSTIN MARTYR (BOOK I PAGE 190)

Early cities were often named after their founders. Cain's first son was named Enoch, and Cain built a city which he called after the name of his son (Gen. 4:17). Sacred Jewish history indicates that even the cities in Canaan, such as Sodom, Gomorrah, Adma and Zeboiim (Gen. 14:2), were actually names of the sons of Canaan, who was the youngest son of Ham (Gen. 10:6).

In a similar fashion, before and after the flood, humanity was so enamored with these large men that they named their idols after the names of the giants and their children. Numerous Roman and Greek gods were connected with the planets and the cosmic heavens:

- Apollo—son of Jupiter (also known as Zeus)

- Artemis—the moon goddess

- Hera—Jupiter's wife (called the queen of heaven)

- Zeus—god of the sky, lightning and thunder

- Ares—the son of Jupiter and Juno

- Poseidon—the brother of Jupiter and Pluto

The ancient people of the Middle East and later Roman-occupied areas were quite familiar with the gods (that were actually angels) who came to Earth, and whose seed birthed the men of renown. They built an elaborate system (a type of genealogical lineage) and attempted to trace back the heavenly visitors as gods over the planets and cosmos. It is possible that fallen angels took upon themselves the names of these planets, and thus the planets were thought to be named after them. This makes sense if we consider that the New Testament indicates there were angels who "did not keep their first estate" (or proper domain - see Jude 6). The angels originally assigned to Earth in human form were considered gods to the pre-flood and post-flood generations.

While the generation of giants in Noah's day would have perished in the flood, and after the flood others would have been slain by David and his men, their *spiritual influence* continued for generations as men carved idols from wood, stone and clay, gave them names, and considered these lifeless objects deities. Idolatry is about worshipping a false god, and this form of iniquity was common after the flood. After the tower of Babel, it spread to the nations.

I have often wondered how a man-made idol of stone or clay could influence a person to build a temple, form a priesthood, and burn incense to that cold, lifeless object. In reality, the ancient worshippers were tapping into the spirit behind the image, as much as the image itself. When we understand that behind these images and names *were once actual demigods,* then we can see how their names and legends built a mythological genealogy that was embellished by future generations and led to the debauchery of idolatry. Satan has always had a desire to be worshipped (Isa. 14:13-14), and even suggested that Christ bow and worship him (Matt. 4:9). Thus, idolatry is about choosing another god besides the true God, which makes all idolatry a form of Satan worship.

Idolatry leads to spiritual bondage, and I believe demonic spirits are assigned to every idol that is worshipped by ignorant individuals. In the middle of the future seven-year Tribulation, the false prophet will make an image of the Antichrist, and through demonic power the image will speak and live. Anyone who refuses to worship the image will be executed by beheading (see Rev. 13:15; 20:4). Idolatry began to manifest following the flood of Noah and continued to spread into Egypt, Assyria, Babylon, Media-Persia, Greece, and Rome. Idolatry will climax with the greatest deception of all time, when a manmade icon will live and speak, and multitudes will worship a demonically-controlled idol.

THE LOT PROPHETIC PARALLELS

Christ compared the events surrounding His return to the days of Noah and Lot (see Luke 17:26-30). All students of prophecy are aware of the Noah-Lot parallels: eating, drinking, marrying, given in marriage, buying, selling, planting, and so forth.

From the conclusion of the flood to Abraham's birth was around 345 years. Giants were on Earth both *before* and *after* the flood (Gen. 6:4). Jewish history and tradition state that after the flood, a second group of angels were sent from heaven to live among men and instruct them in the truth of God, but these also fell into lust, had relations with women, and procreated a second race of giants. This is alluded to in various Jewish writings. According to one tradition, one of the leading angels after the flood was named Azazel. The Book of Enoch (the Ethiopian translation) records when this second group of angels were bound and placed in hell, under God's instruction to one of the seven chief angels named Raphael and Michael the archangel:

> "Further God said to Raphael, 'Bind Azazel by his hands and his feet...And split open the desert which is in Deudael, and throw

him in there. And cover him with darkness; and let him stay there forever...that on the Day of Judgment he may be hurled into the fire.' And God said unto Michael, 'Go inform Shemyaza and the other with him...when all their sons kill each other, and when they see the destruction of their beloved ones, bind them for seventy generations under the hill of the earth until the Day of Judgment...and in those days they will lead them to the abyss of fire.''

The book of Jubilees (called the Lesser Genesis) is a book known in the first century and referred to by numerous early church fathers. The book was utilized by the Essenes, the community of men living in Qumran prior to the destruction of the temple. It is believed to date to about 160 – 150 BC. In the book of Jubilees is another account of the binding of the angels that sinned:

> "And it came to pass when the sons of men began to increase on the earth, and daughters were born to them that in the first year of the jubilee the angels of God looked on them and saw that they were beautiful; and they took wives from them as many as they chose. And they bore them sons: and they became giants...And against the angels He had sent on earth His anger was so great that he uprooted them from their dominion and commanded us to imprison them in the depths of the earth; and behold they are in prison there and separate."
>
> – JUBILEES 5:1-6

The Apostle Peter wrote about the overthrow of Sodom and Gomorrah and how God turned them to ashes as an example to others who would follow after their sins (2 Pet. 2:6). Peter also alluded to the flood of Noah and mentioned that God spared eight souls:

> "For if God did not spare the angels who sinned, but cast them down to hell and delivered them into chains of darkness, to be reserved unto judgment; and did not spare the ancient world, but saved Noah, one of eight people, a preacher of righteousness, bringing in the flood on the world of the ungodly..."
>
> – 2 PETER 2:4-5 (NKJV)

Peter's statement in the Bible agrees with the commentary in these Jewish writings—that angels sinned and now are imprisoned in hell awaiting the judgment (that is, the great white throne judgment, see Revelation 20:11-15).

After the flood, as the population expanded on Earth, there were numerous groups of giants surrounding the Promised Land. The corruption of the human DNA *after the flood* was Satan's second attempt to interfere with God's seed promise in Genesis 3:15, which predicted that the seed of the woman would crush the head of the seed of the serpent. However, following the flood, there was a new level of human seed disruption that entered the biblical and historical record during the time of Abraham and Lot.

A NEW PERVERSION EMERGES

This new iniquity was an odd form of perversion that appears to have emerged, after the flood, in the land of Canaan. The name Canaan was the early name for the land later called Israel that originally stretched from the mountains south in Lebanon, into Canaan Land, and extending south near the Negev Desert. Five cities were built in the southern region of Canaan; four were located in the open plains near the southern end of the Dead Sea, and one small city named Zoar was built on an upper mountain not far from two cities called Sodom and Gomorrah.

Moses narrated the activities and spiritual condition within the city of Sodom. The prophet Ezekiel informed us there were several prominent sins among the inhabitants of Sodom, including pride, fullness of bread (gluttony), an abundance of idleness, and failure to support the poor. They were also haughty (arrogant) and they committed abominations (Ezek. 16:49-50). Ezekiel never elaborates on the specific sins he called abominations. However, Genesis 19 exposes one of the abominations of Sodom. When God sent two angelic beings in the form of human men to personally investigate the moral and spiritual conditions within the city, Lot immediately invited the strangers into his home, not just for hospitality but for their own protection. Once the two strangers were secure behind Lot's door, at sunset the old men and the young men in the city assembled at the door and demanded that Lot release the two men that "we might know them." The word "know" is the same Hebrew word used in Genesis 4:1, "And Adam knew his wife Eve; and she conceived..." This word also is used in the verse, "Cain knew his wife; and she conceived..." (Gen. 4:17) and, "Adam knew his wife again and she bore a son..." (Gen. 4:25). While the Hebrew word *knew*, which is *yada*, can have several meanings, in the context of the men asking for these two strangers in Lot's house, the word "know" is a request to have a sexual encounter with them. With the number of men involved, "the men of Sodom...young and old...from every quarter," the plan of these Sodomites was to gang rape these two men.

If this seems improbable, then read Judges 19, where a man and his concubine spent the night near Jebus (Jerusalem) and at night the men of the city demanded that the owner of the house release the male stranger for their sexual pleasure. They wanted to "know him" (see Judges 19:22). That night the concubine, a young woman traveling with the man, was sent outside the house where she was gang raped all night by men the Bible calls the "sons of Belial," a name referring to perverseness. In both stories the men of the city came out at night like a pack of wild wolves and searched the streets for any stranger to molest. The story in Judges sadly reveals that the young woman died outside the house with her hand on the door (Judges 19:27).

In the beginning, from the time of Adam and the righteous lineage of Seth to Noah, God's first ordained covenant—the covenant of marriage—was honored. Perhaps because of the intermingling of the seed, which would have occurred in Cain's lineage (he is called "of that wicked one," see 1 John 3:12), the idea of sexual perversion was introduced through the fallen angels. Some argue that angels are genderless, and thus they cannot perform that natural function. This is true when they are in a *spirit form*; but when they take upon themselves a flesh nature, they can eat, speak, and perform any function that a normal human can (see Genesis 18). Christ pre-existed with the Father and became robed in a flesh body (called the incarnation). Once He moved into the earthly realm, He was subject to all temptation just as you and I, yet He did not sin (Heb. 4:15). While it remains a mystery how these angels' sins of the flesh occurred, we are told that when we entertain strangers, we could be entertaining angels unaware (Heb. 13:2).

Seed Destroyers

As we understand the importance of the marriage covenant, of a man and woman procreating to conceive sons and daughters, and as we become aware of the adversary's sly methods to hinder God's spiritual purpose for a family, then consider the reason that giants were birthed and men became attracted to men. The battle in Scripture has always been for the *promises* of God. In the parable of the sower (Matthew 13:18-23), the seed is the Word of God, and when the seed in unable to germinate properly in the heart, there is no spiritual growth leading to maturity.

The ultimate purpose of the giant offspring was to corrupt the seed of all men, thus perverting and tainting the "seed of the woman" that was promised to defeat the powers of Satan (see Gen 3:15). The Messiah had to come from a pure bloodline of men and women of faith who believed in the true God and kept His word and commandments. This is one reason God instructed the Israelites not to marry outside their faith and ethnic group following the Exodus.

After the Babylonian captivity, when the Levites and priests returned to Jerusalem, many priests had intermarried with women from foreign nations. Nehemiah demanded they either separate from the women or step down from the priestly ministry, as there could be no mingling of the seed among the priests (see Ezra 10:2-6; Neh. 13:27-31). The Messiah of Israel had to come as a descendant of Abraham through the tribe of Judah and from the house of David. Any disruption of this linage could have marred the redemptive blood covenant and destroyed the promise and the prophecies assigned to Jesus the Messiah.

Satan is a seed killer. This is clearly seen when Pharaoh and Herod both instructed that male infants be slain. Pharaoh saw the growth of Israel and used an after-birth abortion strategy for population control (see Exodus 1). King Herod, on the other hand, was just a bloodthirsty man with no regard for human life. Josephus said he was jealous of his wife and had her murdered, and in anger he killed his two sons. Herod could slay hundreds of infants, age two years and under, and not blink an eye, just as abortionists can rip a baby apart and smile all the way to the bank with no conscience or guilt, even when viewing the remains of the ones they butchered.

More Space Visitors?

Some people have a fascination and even an obsession with aliens and alien abductions. In the ancient writings of the Sumerians are translated clay tablets that indicate a belief that the "gods" (called "kingship") came from the stars or from distant planets to visit and then dwell among mankind. These "gods" were no doubt the angels that God permitted to come to Earth and teach men righteousness, between the time of Enos (Gen. 4:26) and Noah. However, they fell into lust for young women. If "gods" (fallen angels) once came to Earth and are now bound under the earth until the Day of Judgment, could there be something sinister occurring in the supernatural realm with the large number of strange lights, objects, and other weird manifestations occurring throughout the world?

Since the majority of unidentified flying objects began to be spotted after World War II, it is possible that a majority are actually forms of American military technology that are being developed in underground bases. There is, however, an extreme interest in aliens that is spreading throughout the world. While most people consider the alien conspirators an imaginative fringe group, occasionally there are unexplainable incidents that may be a prelude to a clash of the heavenly war which is coming—a war between angels of God and the angels of Satan.

During the first appearance of Christ, angelic visitations increased as angels were seen by Mary, Zachariah, Elizabeth, Joseph, and those at the garden tomb following Christ's resurrection. Two men in white also appeared to Christ's disciples on the Mount of Olives when Christ ascended (Acts 1:10-11). If the same parallels of the season of

Christ's first appearing repeat themselves, we are possibly in for visitations from the spirit world.

ISSUING ESCAPE ORDERS

Noah, Lot, and their families were given a unique opportunity, as God provided a *way of escape* for them and their families. Noah prepared an ark, having ample time to build the ship and collect the food needed to ride out a long storm. Lot, on the other hand, was given a very short warning (about 24 hours) to get as far out of the blast zone as he could. In both instances, severe judgment was restrained until both families were safe at their destination. Noah and seven others were in the ark, and Lot and his two daughters were walking up the mountain toward Zoar. The angels of the Lord confessed they were restrained from releasing the fire on Sodom until Lot was out of the city (Gen. 19:22).

Another often overlooked point is that there were five cities slated for God's judgment: Sodom, Gomorrah, Admah, Zeboiim, and Zoar (see Genesis 14:2). However, when Lot requested to go up the mountain to Zoar, noting that it was a "little city" (Gen. 19:20), the angel then altered the initial plan of destruction, telling Lot, "I will not overthrow this city for which you have spoken" (Gen. 19:21). Lot is called a "righteous man" (2 Pet. 2:7-8) and his right standing with God served as a restrainer against the judgment of God.

Throughout biblical history, the Lord would at times issued a directive for the righteous to leave one location and move to another. Christ warned that the temple and Jerusalem would be destroyed within one generation (Matt 23:34-39). He gave advanced notice of how to escape the destruction when believers saw a particular alignment of events. He said that Jerusalem would be encircled with armies and when you see this, flee out of the city quickly and do not return to your house to take anything out (Luke 21:20-21).

Another example is Paul. Christ's final instruction included the great commission to go into all the world and preach the Gospel to every creature (Mark 16:15). The Apostle Paul exemplified this instruction by traveling and preaching throughout the Roman Empire territory. However, on one occasion the Holy Spirit forbade him from preaching in Asia (Acts 16:6-7). As they made their journey to Mysia and prepared to journey to Bithynia, again the Lord would not release Paul to make the journey. Perhaps this was for his protection or perhaps, as later indicated in the text, God had another assignment for him (see Acts 16:6-12). God knew the danger spots and by revelation of the Spirit instructed Paul to avoid these areas.

In the Lot narrative, the two men (angelic beings) instructed Lot not to remain in the plains, which was at that time a fertile valley at the southern end of the Dead Sea, but to journey up the mountain where he would be preserved from destruction. When the fire fell on Sodom and Gomorrah, Abraham was at that time living on the mountains of Beersheba, an area with wells of water. From the hills of Beersheba, Abraham could see the fire of Sodom as the fireballs came from heaven. He described it as the "smoke of a great furnace" (Gen. 19:28), perhaps indicating what some geologists believe, that the fire was an underground explosion that sent hot lava and magma shooting up in the air and raining down upon the city.

Christ gave the sign (Jerusalem being surrounded) to His disciples and the general direction to flee to the mountains (Matt. 24:16). Lot escaped to the mountains and the ark of Noah rested on the mountains (Gen. 8:4). In the early stages of the future Tribulation, men will hide themselves in the dens and rocks of the mountains (see Rev. 6:15-16). In Lot's time the major cities were in the plains. They provided springs of water and easy access where caravans and travelers could stop in their journey from one location to another. Smaller cities were built on high plateaus, as these were at times more difficult to reach. Two large mountaintop fortresses in Israel are Masada and Gamala, both built on high, natural, rugged mountains, that served in the Roman time as strongholds where Jewish rebels held out for a season against the Roman legions. Mountains paint an imagery of security, versus cities that are built in open valleys.

As the world approaches the hoof beats of the four horseman of the Apocalypse, many of the world's large cities will become so unsafe that some people will stop venturing out after sunset (this is already true in some inner cities). I say this based upon previous patterns. In both the case of Sodom and of the unnamed man with his concubine, the perverted and violent men of the city came out at night, after sunset, to find any stranger they could sexually assault (Gen. 19:4-5; Judges 19:25). Also note that in both instances, the Sodomites were violent and willing to beat down the door of the house to gain access to the men they desired (Gen. 19:9; Judges 19:22) When the angels told Lot they would "abide in the street all night," Lot warned them not to and said they should remain inside the house. Lot knew the danger awaiting them (Gen. 19:2-3).

A large city consists of various nationalities and ethnic groups, diverse religions, high rates of crime, drug and alcohol abuse, and every other form of vice. The smaller rural communities often have the advantage of people knowing their neighbors, protecting each other, and watching their children grow up together in the same schools. Being born in West Virginia and having lived in both smaller mountain towns and larger cities, I can say that the faith of the rural and mountain people runs deeper. Family life is important to them, and their moral standards often differ dramatically from those of the people in America's large cities, especially the West Coast and Northeastern cities. Often the major media outlets of the Northeast appoint themselves the official voice for the American people, falsely believing their opinions represent the majority, and thus attempting to force all—including those who reject their twisted perversion of morality—to accept their ideas.

Clearly, the days of Lot and Noah are being repeated in our time, as predicted by Christ.

CHAPTER 2

DECODING THE
JUDGMENT FILES

ERHAPS THE MOST misunderstood, misrepresented, and controversial phrase in the Christian and secular community is "the judgment of God." Reflecting back on September 11, 2001, when sincere people wanted an explanation for why God would not stop the terrorists, the countless explanations that often contradicted one another demonstrated a high level of ignorance of biblical understanding. Some announced it was an inside job by the CIA to initiate war in the Islamic world. When some Jews did not show up for work at the Twin Towers, the Arab world quickly announced the attack was instigated not by Islamic terrorists, but by covert Israeli Mossad agents posing as Islamic terrorists. Others suggested that, in the case of the Pentagon attack, a plane never hit the building, but was a pre-planned explosion that originated inside the facility. Some continue to allege that the plane over Pennsylvania was shot down by U.S. fighter jets, and did not crash on its own as had been initially reported. The conspiracies almost seemed endless.

Then some questioned: Is this a selective judgment from God upon America's economy? Did God allow America's protective hedge to come down and give the enemy access to perform evil?

When this question became the topic on internet blogs, radio programs, and even secular cable news, the majority of respondents were appalled at the very idea that God would permit the attack, when so many innocent people were killed. One area where controversy and ignorance reign is the understanding of the judgment of God, and how and why it is released.

FIVE IMPORTANT WORDS

In the New Testament the word judgment is mentioned seventy-six times, with a host of different meanings. One reference speaks of the judgment seat, which is the large bema where the Judean Governor Pilate sat when Jesus came before him for a public trial (Matt. 27:19). Paul spoke of a future heavenly judgment where all believers will give an account of their works and words, called the "judgment seat of Christ" (Rom. 14:10). In Greek this is called the "bema", a word referring to the raised platform where the judges sat, and where the winners of the games would stand when receiving their rewards. This judgment is in heaven and is mentioned in Revelation 11:18. A second judgment occurs in the heavenly temple at the end of the thousand-year reign of Christ, and is called the great white throne judgment (Rev. 20:11-12).

In Acts chapter 5, a married couple in the church, Ananias and Sapphira, conspired to defraud the Lord with their financial giving, and the Holy Spirit initiated a judgment where both were slain for their lie. The most noted example of the *wrath and judgment of God* being released upon the earth is found in Revelation, where John saw both cosmic calamities and natural disasters impacting the waters, rivers, cities, and food supplies over much of the earth. These judgments are specifically identified as the wrath of God (Rev. 16:1), the wrath of the Lamb (Rev. 6:16), and the judgments of God (Rev. 15:4; 16:7; 19:2). The word used for God's judgments in Revelation 15:4 is the Greek word *dikaioma*, and alludes to a statute or a decision that has been decreed. In Revelation 16 these decreed judgments are being released globally. The word judgments in Revelation 16:7 and 19:2 is *krisis*, and alludes to a separation leading to a judgment.

God's judgment can be understood by comparing it to criminal evidence given to a forensic specialist who will examine the details and find proof that can be used at the trial against the plaintiff. The word *krisis* involves a decision by a tribunal to bring justice after there has been a decree of guilt.

There are numerous examples of God *weighing* a person, a city, a nation, or the world to determine their guilt or innocence related to His laws and covenants. For example, King Belshazzar of Babylon hosted a midnight party where he supplied wine from the golden vessels seized from Jerusalem's sacred temple and praised Babylon's false gods. Suddenly God crashed the festivities when He wrote on the wall the words Daniel translated: "You have been weighed in the balances and found wanting" (Dan. 5:27). Daniel stood before the king that evening and predicted his empire would fall that very night to the Persians (which did occur). Daniel also reminded this proud king that, years before, his arrogant relative Nebuchadnezzar had been weighed and God allowed the king to experience a complete mental breakdown that lasted seven years (see Daniel 4).

In biblical history, numerous cities were placed on God's divine hit list because of the evil, perversion, and iniquity of their inhabitants. Sodom and Gomorrah were twin cities that were consumed to ashes as their iniquities had reached into heaven (see Gen. 19). Jonah was assigned to journey into Assyria and warn the city of Nineveh that their people had forty days to repent, or else destruction was set for them (see the book of Jonah). The people of Jerusalem broke God's laws, and the city was invaded by the Babylonians. Tens of thousands of Jews were sent into captivity for seventy years. Generations after the Jews returned and resettled the land, the Romans occupied Israel. Christ gave a stern warning that Jerusalem would be taken again, the temple destroyed, and the people scattered (see Matthew 23:34-39; 24:1-3). This time the reason for Jerusalem's destruction was that their religious leaders had shed the innocent blood of the righteous, including several noted prophets (Matt. 23:35).

In the future Tribulation, the city ruling over the kings of the earth will be destroyed in one hour. The world will be in shock as kings and rulers weep when the smoke rises from the devastation (see Revelation 17 and 18). The reason for God's retribution is vengeance upon this city for slaying the saints and prophets, as the blood of the righteous souls in heaven cries out to God to avenge them of their violent deaths at the hands of evil men (see Rev. 6:10; 17:6).

People who mock or ignore prophetic warnings cannot rationalize why a good God would allow any form of judgment. Even some biblically literate believers think that God, in His love and mercy, would never allow anything bad to occur on earth that would take the lives of many people.

DISCERNING JUDGMENT

The first step is to actually discern what *is* and what *is not* God's judgment. During the biblical judgments, the forces of nature are often released—wind (tornados, hurricanes, storms); earth (earthquakes); fire (volcanoes); and water (rain and floods, along with the lack of rain leading to droughts and famines).

The global flood in Noah's time was certainly a divine sentence, decreed by God to purge the planet of the vile corruption that entrenched mankind. The waters covered the highest mountain for 150 days, and it took over six months for the waters to recede. Afterwards, God set His rainbow in the heaven as a token that the earth would never be destroyed again by water (see Genesis 6-8). I believe one of the end-time prophetic parallels with the days of Noah must include water, since this was the main element of judgment in Noah's time.

In the Genesis account of the flood, water was released from above and below. The water from above was the rain that fell continually for forty days and nights (Gen. 7:4). The water gushing from below was unleashed when the fountains of the deep were broken (Gen. 7:11). These fountains were the subterranean waters under the crust of the earth that gushed forth when the earth's crust began to crack. This created immediate flooding, and as the crust under the seas cracked, the coastal areas would have experienced tsunami type waves.

Currently we are seeing two extremes throughout the world: drought and floods. For example, in the United States, California has experienced a four-year drought where the rivers, lakes, and outdoor water supplies are drying up. However, toward the east, the land has been drenched by torrential rains that flooded much of the state. Some areas were hit with three feet of water in a few hours! This reminds me of the imagery of the windows of heaven opening and torrential rains pouring down.

The second parallel connecting Noah's day and our time is the fountains of the deep sending water through the cracks of the earth to create havoc on the population. This imagery brings to mind the deadly tsunamis in both Indonesia (2004) and Japan (2011), which did untold damage and cost hundreds of thousands of lives.

THE SEA AND WAVES WILL ROAR

In the end time prophetic signs Christ gave to His followers, I believe the prophetic warning found in Luke 21:25 might cryptically be referring to a tsunami. There are specific signs connected with the seas (oceans) prior to the return of Christ:

> "And there shall be signs in the sun, and in the moon, and in the stars; and upon the earth distress of nations, with perplexity; the sea and the waves roaring."

Other translations of this verse say:

> "Dismay among nations, in perplexity at the roaring of the sea and the waves."
>
> – LUKE 21:25 (NASU)

> "Distress (trouble and anguish) of nations in bewilderment and perplexity [without resources, left wanting, embarrassed, in doubt, not knowing which way to turn] at the roaring (the echo) of the tossing of the sea."
>
> – LUKE 21:25 (AMP)

> "Perplexity at the roaring of the sea and the waves."
>
> – LUKE 21:25 (NAS)

> "And down here on earth the nations will be in turmoil, perplexed by the roaring seas and strange tides."
>
> – LUKE 21:25 (NLT)

The 1611 King James translation uses the word roaring to describe the sound coming from the sea and waves. The Greek word here for roaring is *echeo*, from which we derive the word echo. An echo is not just a sound or a noise; it is sound waves that are reflected off a surface back to the listener. Twenty-four hours after the Indonesian tsunami, survivors began posting their eye-witness accounts of what they heard and saw prior to the high waves crashing violently onto the coastal regions. They described a strange "roaring sound coming from the sea." This strange roaring sound may well describe the same noise Christ spoke of in His prophetic discourse.

My Own Visions of the Tsunamis

Before sharing my own dreams and visions of possible tsunamis in America, let me preface my remarks with some important statements.

First, in each of the night dreams and visions, I was never given a set timeframe in which they might occur. Things you see in the Spirit today might not actually unfold for many years. In 1996 I saw a vision of the World Trade Center shrouded in black, with five grayish tornados spinning off the towers. Five years later, when the planes struck the Twin Towers and they collapsed, I saw those same grayish pillars of smoke moving in a fast spinning motion down the streets of New York City. It was five years and three months before the vision manifested in the natural.

Secondly, these visions and dreams can refer to a natural tsunami, such as struck Indonesia and Japan, and this is the first interpretation I would present. However, they can also be symbolic of political or economic storms that bring devastation or some type of destruction to an area. In the Bible a sudden storm can represent numerous types of difficulties. Thus, my first interpretation is to take these literally, and my second would be to say they reveal some form of trouble in the nation.

I am often hesitant to share information about locations, seeing that some tend to panic and become fearful, and might make rash decisions based upon a warning. However, a person must seek God earnestly and find His will and not be moved by fear or circumstances, as He will never leave or forsake us. He will either give us a plan of escape, as with Lot; or He will give us the grace to go through the storm, as with Noah.

TSUNAMIS — THREE REGIONS IN AMERICA

During one of my night visions I was near a coastal city, in a duplex on the second floor, overlooking the city on one side and the Atlantic Ocean on the other. Looking toward the city, I saw small dark clouds forming and knew a storm was brewing. I saw a woman taking pictures and yelled at her to get to safety as a storm was coming. Turning toward the ocean I saw a beautiful bridge connecting the city with another section of land. I saw a green interstate sign that simply read "Charleston," and I knew it referred to Charleston, South Carolina.

Immediately I saw a ghostly image of the Twin Towers arise from the sea and slowly vaporize into the sky, like smoke rising and dissipating. Immediately I saw the bridge shake, which was followed by a massive wave that looked to be possibly sixty to a hundred feet high. When the wave rose, it moved swiftly toward the bridge, which suddenly began to crumble into the water. I yelled to my family in the duplex to get to safety, as the waves were going to crash into the second floor.

Months later, a second dream followed in which I was on the west coast of the United States preparing to fly out on a small plane from a regional airport. In the plane with me was a pastor whose church is in the state of California. As the plane lifted into the air, I looked back and saw the ocean and a massive wave that was rising higher and higher into the air, moving toward the coast. I remember yelling to the pilot to get the plane up higher and do so fast to prevent this wave from taking down the plane. We escaped, but I looked back and realized the entire lowland would be covered in water, including thousands of homes, businesses, and people. It was a very troubling dream and I awoke, unable to go back to sleep.

I believe the third incident I saw connects with the vision of the east coast storm, as it was similar to the night vision of the duplex on the coast. In this experience, I was in the two-story home of a retired minister who lives near the water just outside of Baltimore, Maryland.

We were downstairs talking, when suddenly water came from nowhere and began pouring into his house. I said, "Oh my, this is the result of a tsunami." I grabbed food and bottled water, and yelled for everyone to get upstairs to the second floor. As we rushed upstairs, the water began to swirl downstairs and rise quickly up the steps. I attempted to find an attic that we could climb into. This was the third dream or night vision I experienced of a tsunami.

These dreams continued for many months. In another I saw huge amounts of water cover the earth, like a flood, and a voice said, "This will be global." I recall seeing water pour over a region, as I climbed into a spot of safety carved out of white stone (white in the Bible is righteousness and the stone is a picture of Christ, or being hidden in Christ).

On one occasion, when I shared on our ministry Facebook page a brief word on one of these night visions, I was stunned to read over sixty comments from different people who experienced the same type of warning—all having seen tsunamis strike coastal areas of the United States. Over a period of two years, in my troubling visions and spiritual dreams, I have seen water coming in from three directions—the Pacific Ocean, the Atlantic Ocean, and the Gulf of Mexico.

Our generation is running on a path parallel with the days of Noah. God's rainbow covenant promises us that never again will the world be completely destroyed by a flood. However, the sea and waves roaring indicates a Messianic sign, and the regional floods and coastal destructions by tsunamis can fulfill both the word of Christ and the patterns of prophecy.

JUDGMENT FROM THE WIND

It is amazing to me how wind can form a tornado or a hurricane, spinning with such speed that 18-wheelers are tossed like match-box cars, and an object as tiny as straw from a broom can be thrust several inches into a telephone pole. In Genesis 11, Nimrod (who was believed by some Jewish rabbis to have been a giant), made a tall tower with brick and mortar that would reach into heaven (Gen. 11:4). According to the Jewish historian Josephus, the famed Tower of Babel came crashing down when the Lord sent a mighty wind of destruction:

> "Men built a high tower but the gods sent storms of wind and overthrew the tower, and gave everyone their particular language; and for this reason it was the city of Babylon."
>
> – JOSEPHUS

The destruction of the tower was not a natural phenomenon, but was considered an act of God against the rebels constructing a man-made skyscraper. Some archeologists believe that the tower was actually an ancient ziggurat, which was not so much designed to reach heaven. It was (according to Josephus) to be high enough that, if God chose to destroy the plains of Shinar with flood waters, the leaders would get to the top and survive. Some also suggest that the top of the tower was a place where the stars could be observed and worshipped. Whatever the purpose, post-flood men felt they were unrestrained from living and building as they wished; however, God in His displeasure sent a violent wind that tore down man's vain accomplishments.

JUDGMENT USING FIRE

Four major judgments in the Bible linked with fire include the fire from heaven that consumed Sodom and Gomorrah, and turned the cities to ashes (see Gen 19; 2 Pet 2:6). When Israel rebelled against Moses' authority, God sent a fire in the wilderness and consumed the rebels in a moment's time (Num. 11:1-3). Both the walls and the temple in Jerusalem were burnt with fire twice: once by the Babylonians (425 BC) and once by the Romans (AD 70). Another judgment by fire will happen during the Great Tribulation, when the Lord will permit hail and fire to be part of His sentence upon the unrepentant world (Rev. 8:7).

In apocalyptic literature there are angels that control the winds (Rev. 7:1) and an angel positioned in heaven who oversees fire (Rev. 14:18). John also described an angel who has authority to control the sun (Rev. 16:8). Angels can withhold rains on Earth and have power to shut the heavens and initiate extended droughts that will dry up rivers (Rev. 16:12). During the apocalypse, when angels begin to manifest judgments from God's heavenly temple, there is often a manifestation of lightning and thunder from God's throne (Rev. 4:5; 8:5; 11:19; 16:18).

All the rules of nature and the cosmos operate by divine order established by God at creation, as God is presently upholding all things by the word of His power, and by Him all things consist (Col. 1:17; Heb. 11:3). However, it does appear that God has assigned mighty angels over certain aspects of His creation, including earth, wind and fire; and as God chooses, He can commission an angel to impact a specific region on earth using these elements.

WHAT IS AND IS NOT FROM GOD?

The task is to discern what is and is not a judgment from God. Using the Scriptures, it is evident that not all wind, storms, fires, floods, and earthquakes are judgments from the Lord.

With earthquakes, we see both the natural shakings (the earthquakes that are from the Lord but do not harm people) and earthquakes that are a sign of God's wrath and bring devastation. Earthquakes are noted throughout Scripture. However, when an earthquake from the Lord occurred where a prophet was present, it never harmed anybody.

When Moses was atop Mount Sinai, the entire mountain quaked with thunder and smoke; yet no one at the base of the hill was physically harmed or slain by falling rocks (see Exodus 19). When Elijah entered the cave on Mount Horeb, the rocks were rent; but the Lord was not in the quake and Elijah was never harmed (1 Kings 19:11). A third example was at Christ's death and during His resurrection, when earthquakes shook Jerusalem with no reports of any injuries or deaths. In fact, the moment of Christ's death, the rocks were rent the same time the veil in the temple was torn, sending spiritual conviction to the Roman Centurion at the foot of the cross who confessed, "Truly this was the Son of God" (Matt. 27:54). In Acts 16, Paul and Silas conducted a midnight worship service while chained in a Roman prison. Their duet was interrupted by a shaking—an earthquake that caused chains to fall off and iron prison doors to jerk off their hinges. These were stone prison walls and this earthquake should have caused major damage and even death; yet not one person was injured or killed.

While these are examples of natural earthquakes as well as those sent from God that caused no injuries or deaths, there are earthquakes that are a sign of God's judgment being enacted after a heavenly tribunal decreed a sentence upon the guilty. Untold millions of men, women, and children were carried under the waters of Noah's flood, and the opening of the fountains of the great deep would have caused a shift in the plates of the earth under the seas. On one occasion in the wilderness, Korah and 250 leaders sparked a rebellion against Moses and Aaron. To confirm God's will, the Almighty split the ground, sending Korah and his entire house into pits under the earth's crust (see Numbers 16). In the latter part of the Great Tribulation, God will permit the greatest earthquake in world history that will cause the cities of the nations to fall (Rev. 16:19). The Scripture indicates that earthquakes *at times* can be a visible manifestation of God's wrath being executed in the form of a shaking that impacts men, cities and nations.

DISCERNING THE WIND

There are things God is in, and things He is not in. Wind is a common phenomenon. We appreciate a breeze on a hot day, but despise the bitter cold wind on a winter day. Wind is also considered a manifestation of God. In Acts 2, on the festival of Pentecost, a mighty rushing wind blew into the room where Christ's followers were gathered. Cloven tongues as of fire danced upon them, transforming the speech of these commoners and initiating a new baptism in the Holy Spirit (Acts 2:1-4). God was in this wind!

During Christ's ministry, a late night boat ride on the Sea of Galilee turned into a near disaster as high waves and strong winds suddenly hit the small ship. Jesus stood and rebuked the winds and waves, and brought calm to the storm (Matt. 8:26). This storm was not from God, as Christ would have never rebuked His Father. This tempest was not necessarily from Satan, because storms like this occur continually on the Sea of Galilee when the winds pick up and whip across the mountains. This was a natural, yet dangerous storm that was reduced to a breeze when Christ exercised His spiritual authority.

Fire is another example. Elijah confronted 450 false prophets on Mount Carmel with one condition: the God that can answer by fire is the real God. When Elijah prayed, the fire of the Lord fell (1 Kings 18:38). On the opposing end, in the wilderness, several sons of the high priest decided to offer their own fire and God called it "strange fire". The Lord was not in the strange fire, and to prove He wasn't, He slew these priests who built their own fire and claimed it was from God (Num. 3:1-4).

These examples show that in the case of storms, floods, earthquakes, tsunamis, and other natural disasters, believers must exercise discretion and discernment when publically announcing the event was a judgment or warning from God. In fact, some early insurance policies stated that trees falling on your house may be deemed "an act of God," thus exempting them from paying any damages. Throughout history, God has been blamed for things He was actually not part of.

AMERICA'S BREACH IN THE WALL

When Jeremiah wrote Lamentations, he penned a thought that brings to mind the danger America is facing:

> "The kings of the earth, and all the inhabitants of the world, would not have believed that the adversary and the enemy should have entered the gates of Jerusalem."
>
> – LAMENTATIONS 4:12 (KJV)

In Jeremiah's time, Jerusalem was a city secured by high stone walls, with huge wooden gates wrapped in iron erected at the city's main entrances. On top of the walls were watchmen, along with gate-keepers. The city sat upon a hill with deep gorges surrounding the walls, making it difficult for any advancing army to fight an uphill battle against the Israelites. The east, west, and southern sides of the walled fortress were almost impossible for any army to penetrate. However, the foundation of the northern wall was at ground level, and each time the city was breached, it was from the north. The Israelites and foreign kings felt the city was impregnable. But Jeremiah said that, because of the sins of the prophets and iniquities of the priests and the shedding of the blood of righteous men, the anger of the Lord was kindled against Jerusalem (Lam. 4:12-16).

Walls and gates are the hedge placed between the people and their enemies that prevent the adversary from entering the safety of the villages within. The gates of the city are the access points in and out of the city. At night the city gates were secured with iron bars and, at times, with locks to keep unwanted individuals or bands of evil men from entering the city. Two dangers existed for any ancient city. First was a breach in the wall or an opening that left the city unprotected from intruders. The second was an opening in the gate, making it possible for an adversary to easily walk into the city.

According to the book of Job, hedges are invisible to the naked eye; but when God assigns a hedge of protection, it covers a wide gambit of things. Job's hedge protected him, his children, his livestock, and the houses in which the family dwelt (Job. 1:1-10). This hedge was designed and controlled by God Himself. Satan said to God, "You have put a hedge around him...on every side" (Job 1:10). Only when God gave Satan permission to test Job was the hedge removed (Job 1:11-12). At the conclusion of the story, God reset boundaries restraining Satan's assault and also released a double blessing on Job for his integrity and faithfulness (see Job 42).

An example of walls being breached is the ancient fortified city of Jericho. Archeologists excavated the ruins of Jericho and discovered numerous levels of occupation covering thousands of years. The city from Joshua's time was constructed with layers of stone on the outside to provide a strong defense against an attacking army. When Jericho was seized by the Israelites, the walls of the city were supernaturally breached as they collapsed when Israel shouted on the seventh day (see Joshua 6).

Two interesting facts may reveal why God chose to collapse Jericho's walls (create a breach) and thus give Israel access to the city. Years ago I was given one of the original bricks from Jericho, one made of baked mud and straw. I noticed small pieced of bone within the brick, which

I thought odd and assumed it was animal bone. However, my tour guide pointed out that a large clay jar was discovered embedded within the walls of the ancient city. Inside were the brittle bones of what appeared to be an infant. One man who excavates in the region told my guide that he believed some builder of Jericho placed human infant bones in the walls as a form of protection, assuming their god would secure a watch over their city. This would be similar to the Canaanites worshiping the idol Moloch, who would pass their children through the fire as a form of sacrifice and appeasement for the favor of this brass idol (see Lev. 20:2-5).

Of over thirty Canaanite cities Israel conquered under Joshua, this was the only city in which the walls collapsed, giving Israel immediate access to everyone living within the secured walls. It is possible that God sent a judgment against the *walls* because those clay bricks concealed a horrible sin of shedding the innocent blood of infants, and then using the remains of the dead within the bricks.

THE SUPREME COURT BREACH

On June 26, 2015, the United States Supreme Court issued a ruling that affirmed same sex marriage in all fifty states. The decision split the nation, with multitudes claiming this a great day in America and a victory for civil rights. The other half were grieved and aware of the biblical danger America now faced. The four dissenting justices released written warnings of the repercussions and possible dangers ahead, especially for anyone opposing the homosexual agenda.

The danger was not just in the court legalizing a sin that God classifies as an abomination; the danger was also that they claimed to use the Constitution as a guideline for their decision. The founders penned three major documents upon which the foundation of our republic stands: the Constitution, the Bill of Rights, and the Declaration of Independence. The motivation for writing these documents was freedom from the tyrannical power of the kings of England, and the founders compared their struggle to the biblical narrative of Israel being delivered from the bondage of Egypt and the Pharaoh who ruled over them. The moral, judicial, and religious freedom rules they included were based upon the founders' careful study of previous empires (Greece and Rome) and centered upon certain laws given to Moses in the Torah. President Harry Truman commented that our founding documents were based upon the Torah, Psalms, and the four Gospels.

For the majority of the U.S. Supreme Court justices to use those biblically-based documents to justify a decision that is contrary to Scripture is close to blaspheming God, His Word, and His name. It was God Himself who warned, "Thou shalt not lie with mankind as with woman kind; this is an abomination" (Lev. 18:22), and "If a man lie also with mankind, as he lieth with a woman, both of them hath committed an abomination..." (Lev. 20:13). The Almighty went so far as to mark such immoral men as "sons of Belial" (Judg. 20:13; 1 Sam. 2:12). Scholars note that the name *Belial* refers to a useless person— one who is good for nothing and morally base.

Ancient Israel discovered the danger of breaching a promise from God after He instructed them to leave Egypt and repossess the land promised to Abraham through the Abrahamic covenant. Despite God's word, the ten unbelieving spies corrupted the faith of an esti-mated two million people. The result of their unbelief was that God sent them on a journey—in circles—through a desert for forty years. That was one year for each of the forty days the spies were in the land. God called their actions "a breach of promise" (Num. 14:34).

The breach warning is not just on a national level. Solomon warned in Proverbs that, "...perverseness [of the tongue] is a breach in the spirit" (Prov. 15:4). The meaning of the Hebrew word for breach is *a fracture that leads to ruin*. Isaiah gave a strong message to Israel, exposing them as "lying children, children that will not hear the law of the Lord, and who say to the prophets, do not prophesy unto us right things, speak unto us smooth things; prophesy deceits" (Isa. 30:9-10).

Because they broke God's covenant, Israel would experience an inva-sion from a foreign nation—a warning predicted by true prophets, but that nobody believed would occur. The Lord warned them "Therefore this iniquity shall be to you as a breach ready to fall, swelling out in a high wall, whose breaking cometh suddenly at an instant" (Isa. 30:13).

The Babylonians did breach the walls of Jerusalem and thirty days later entered the city and sealed the doom of the temple and Jerusalem.

The date on the Hebrew calendar when the walls of Jerusalem were breached was the 9th of Thammuz. It was ironic that Friday morning, June 26th, the day the secular media announced the Supreme Court's decision on same sex marriage, was the 9th of Thammuz on the Jewish calendar. The morning of that announcement, I sensed that a breach had come to America and our protective hedge that had restrained evil, stopped judgments, and prevented economic collapse was now breached. We are weaker for breaking God's marriage covenant between one man and one woman and, for the demands of the people, that we affirm and legalize that which grieves God.

The prophet Jeremiah wrote that when Babylon invaded Jerusalem, the Lord's people were "broken with a great breach, with a very grievous blow" (Jer. 14:17). By the time of Jeremiah, Israel's cup of iniquity was full to the point that the Lord told Jeremiah that, if Moses or even the prophet Samuel were alive at that moment and attempted to make intercession for the rebellious house of Judah, God would no longer hear their pleas for mercy (Jer. 15:1). Israel's countless years of rebellion, worship of idols, and disobedience to God's law so provoked the Lord that He assigned four forms of adversity that would impact them and their nation (see Jer. 15:3).

Israel's problem was national arrogance among the prophets, priests and kings, who concocted their own theory that Israel and Jerusalem were God's nation and city; thus the Lord would never allow any form of destruction. Jeremiah understood the covenant God made with Abraham for the land (of Israel) and David's everlasting covenant for the city, and he petitioned God saying, "...break not thy covenant with us" (Jer. 14:21).

THE JUDGMENT TRIGGER

There are several purposes for any type of judgment striking the earth. When great evil and wickedness occurs in a region, such as during the days of Noah and Lot, the judgment is directed toward the instigators and participants of the evil. Since evil, wickedness, and criminal activity can only manifest through the minds and hearts of people whose negative actions impact others, the removal of the key promoters of wickedness weakens the influence of the wicked. The fiery judgment of Sodom removed *two generations*—the *old men* and the *young men* (Gen. 19:4) for a specific reason. Had the older men lived, they would have returned to their sin and passed it to the next generation. Had the young men survived, the sin would have also been passed to the next generation, as the iniquities of the fathers can be visited upon the third and fourth generation of those who hate the Lord (see Exod. 20:5; 34:7).

One key that will unlock the door of judgment is when the *cup of iniquity is full*. God revealed the future of Abraham's descendants and spoke of a time they would be in captivity (in Egypt) and later be brought out by God's power:

> "But in the fourth generation they shall come here again: for the iniquity of the Amorites is not yet full."
>
> – GEN. 15:16 (NKJV)

The Amorites were a nomadic people who descended from Canaan (Gen. 14:7) and originated in the Assyrian area, who lived in Syria and the land that today is known as Israel, including the Judean hill country (Deut. 1:7). The Amorites had two noted kings, both of whom were giants—Og, the king of Bashan (whose bed was over 13 feet long—Deut. 3:11) and Sihon, who ruled land on the west side of the Jordan River (Deut. 31:4).

God said the judgment would come when the iniquity of the Amorites was full or complete (Gen. 15:16). Oddly, the Hebrew word for full is *shalem*, which is a word for *complete*, but also carries the idea of peace or security. The idea here is that as long as there is resistance to sin and iniquity, there is an opportunity for grace and mercy to be released. However, once the sins and iniquity have become acceptable, and people feel at peace living in sin and ignoring repentance, then judgment is released. It is the remnant's resistance against iniquity that has given no peace to the instigators of wickedness. However, if and when the church chooses to be peaceable toward sin and accept iniquity, then the cup is full and God releases judgment.

This observation is significant when understanding the timing of the future Great Tribulation. We are presently in the church age or the dispensation of the grace of God. The message, "repent for the kingdom is at hand," is being spread throughout the world. However, as time passes and sin becomes more common and acceptable, people no longer see a reason to repent, as they see nothing they are doing wrong. During the Tribulation, when judgments are erupting all around, John noted three times that "men repented not" (Rev. 9:20; 16:9; 16:11). The time will come when people will know that God is sending His judgments upon them; however, they will refuse to humble themselves and turn from their wickedness.

Presently, there is a remnant in America that understands the consequences of mocking God's covenants and rejecting His Word. This *resisting remnant* is continually seeking God's face for mercy, and mercy has been extended to this nation despite bad leaders, bad decisions, and bad laws. However, this season of mercy can lead spiritually blind leaders to assume that their decisions carry no negative impact. They can even be deceived into believing that God is smiling upon their decisions and actions. In reality, America is hanging over the abyss of economic collapse, natural disaster, and destruction by one thread of mercy in the hands of God, who is hearing cries from His chosen to restrain the judgment while they are still on the earth.

The catching away of the true, overcoming believers will occur in the *fullness of time* (see Eph. 1:9-10), when the cup of mercy is empty and the cup of iniquity is full. As a traveling evangelist, I see fewer sinners truly repenting, and I have observed callousness in the hearts of the unconverted. When the eyes of the Lord search the whole earth and see that the doors of the people's hearts are shut and repentance is resisted, then the end will come.

Another point that identified the release of judgment in Sodom was a statement the Lord made to Abraham, when the Lord concluded a divine investigation that sealed the fate of the four cities of the plain. God said to Abraham:

> "Because the cry of Sodom and Gomorrah is great, and because their sin is very grievous; I will go down now and see whether they have done altogether according to the cry of it, which is come unto me..."
>
> – GENESIS 18:20-21 (KJV)

Once the two angels (who appeared as men) saw that the men of Sodom attempted to beat down the door to gain access to them, the angels turned to Lot and announced, "For we will destroy this place, because the cry of them is waxen great before the face of the Lord..." (Gen. 19:13). When God used the word *cry* in 18:20, the Hebrew is *za'aq*, and means a loud outcry or a shriek. When the angels said the "cry is waxen great" (19:13), the word cry here in Hebrew is *tsa'aqah*, and refers to *loud shrieks*. Who were the people crying out in Sodom, whose cries reached the ears of God in His heavenly temple? In Proverbs 21:13, it speaks of the "cry of the poor" which is the word *za'aq*. Ezekiel alludes to the sins of Sodom and indicated they mistreated the poor (Ezek. 16:49). There are stories in sacred Jewish history that expose how the poor were abused and even slain in Sodom.

After years of reading Scriptures on Sodom and studying Jewish history and tradition, it is clear that not only was the sexual immorality significant, but the mistreatment of strangers and the poor was also a mark against them. It is quite likely that those shrieks came from individuals in Sodom who were victims of rape, incest, and abuse, and who had nobody to defend or protect them from these evil individuals. This hardened attitude is seen when Lot begs the Sodomite mob to leave the two strangers alone. The perversion was so inbred that these old and young men actually threatened to do worse to Lot than they were planning to do to these two men, if Lot didn't follow through with their demands (see Gen. 19:9). These perverted men were willing to threaten a righteous man, break down his door, and gang rape two strangers. The cries of victims, past and present, had gone up, and now God Himself was preparing a divine assault to remove the people and the cities from the earth. *No one repented in Sodom and the city was happy and at peace with iniquity.* In fact, when Lot warned his sons-in-law to get out of the city, they mocked him (Gen. 19:14). They took it as some type of joke.

The prophetic parallel of our time is that there will be both believers and sinners who, instead of paying attention to the warnings, will mock prophetic warnings. Just as Peter predicted, in the last days scoffers will come and say, "Where is the promise of His coming? For since the fathers fell asleep, all things continue *as they were* from the beginning of creation." When believers become mockers and sinners become unrepentant, that is when the restraint is removed and judgment arrives. In the days of Moses, Israel took back the land of Abraham from the Amorites, destroyed their two giant kings, and settled in the land. The cup of iniquity was now full.

WHEN BLOOD CRIES OUT

According to Scripture, God's judgment is poured out on certain cities and entire nations for shedding innocent blood. What is innocent blood? When two nations are at war, soldiers from both sides enter the defensive and offensive arenas as they defend their territory and engage the enemy in warfare. When soldiers in battle defend the rights and freedoms of the innocent against the militants, terrorists, and dictators who are bent on killing the innocent, this is not evil; this is justice. Shedding innocent blood, however, is when a person with evil intent willfully takes the life of an innocent person.

At least thirty-four prophets are mentioned in the Bible and half of those have books included in the Bible. Jesus told His disciples that Jerusalem would be destroyed within one generation because their ancestors had slain righteous people, including Zechariah, who was murdered between the temple's porch and altar. Christ gave the primary reason for God releasing this punishment on the holy city— because of their shedding of righteous blood (see Matt. 23:29-37). The temple and Jerusalem's destruction did occur about thirty-eight years later in AD 70, at the hands of the Roman Tenth Legion.

Moving forward into the future, John saw a vision in heaven of souls who had been slain for the Word of God and for their testimony, all of whom were resting in paradise until their fellow servants would be slain (see Rev.6:9-11). These had been martyred on Earth for standing for Christ. This is occurring now throughout the world, especially among Christians in the Middle East. Later John saw the utter destruction of Mystery Babylon, the city "ruling over the kings of the earth." The reason for the annihilation of this city was her guilt from shedding the blood of prophets and saints (Rev 18:24). Judgment eventually comes because of the cries of the innocent, the righteous, and the saints.

The idea that blood cries out is not an imaginary theory. The first murder in world history was Cain killing his brother Abel because he was jealous over Abel's favor with God. Cain attempted to hide the body in the ground, and God visited Cain and asked, "Where is Abel your brother?" Cain replied, "I do not know. Am I my brother's keeper?" God then told Cain, "The voice of your brother's blood cries to me from the ground" (Gen. 4:5-10). The word cries is *tsa'aq*, again a word for a shrieking outcry. It is a mystery how God can hear the voice concealed in the blood, but this verse indicates that He does. Imagine the millions of aborted infants, murder victims, and innocent men and women who have died at the hands of criminals, terrorists, and other wicked people, as the voice of their blood is lifted to the throne of God.

WHAT DETERMINES THE MOMENT OF JUDGMENT?

Two points are very clear as it relates to the judgment of God on a people or a nation. First, God always gives people multiple opportunities to repent before the angels of judgment are released. It is said this way: God visits in mercy before He strikes in judgment. The mercy visitation is designed as motivation toward repentance, as He always wants people to return to Him. If mercy is rejected and iniquity is accepted as an alternative choice or the new normal, then the mercy cycle begins to fade as warnings are released. Noah was warned 120 years before the flood, Lot was warned twenty-four hours before Sodom was burned, and the citizens of Jerusalem were warned thirty-eight years before the city's actual destruction.

Warnings can manifest through preaching, through dreams and visions, angelic visitations, or a manifestation of the vocal gifts of the Holy Spirit—all of which are biblical and can be activated according to the will of God. If warnings are rejected, God will lift His hand of protection and allow the release of selective judgment in an effort to grab the attention of the people or the nation, so that they will turn toward God and accept His forgiveness and mercy. There is also a spiritual principle that, before any major judgment strikes, those with ears to hear what the Spirit is saying will often be given a window of opportunity to escape the danger zone and move to another location.

Two examples are when Lot departed from Sodom and quickly journeyed up the mountain to Zoar, away from the burning cities. The second is when Christians, a few years prior to Jerusalem's destruction, heeded the words of Christ when He warned that, when you see Jerusalem surrounded by armies, get out of the city and flee to the mountains (Luke 21:21). Numerous Christians escaped the city and traveled to Pella, a region on the other side of the Jordan River, where they were given asylum. Over time, they built a Christian community while Jerusalem was reduced to rubble.

Depending upon the level of iniquity and its impact upon a region, the warning indicators can be either *long* or *brief*. It appears that if the judgment is localized (such as with Sodom), then the time from the warning to the actual act of judgment is brief. In Lot's situation, the coming judgment would impact four cities, and he had only one day to prepare to get out. With Noah, the destruction was worldwide and involved millions of souls; thus the warning was extended for over a hundred years. The time between Christ's prediction and the actual destruction of Jerusalem and the temple was about thirty-eight years (AD 32 to AD 70). However, Christ did say it would occur within a generation (Matt. 23:36; 24:34).

Perhaps the reason the destruction came so swiftly was because, at Christ's trial, Pilate declared him an innocent man and washed his hands before the mob, indicating that he refused to participate in the shedding of innocent blood. The religious leaders yelled back at Pilate, "His [Christ's] blood be upon us and our children" (Matt. 27:25).

The devout Pharisees knew the Mosaic Law against shedding innocent blood and how the *land* comes under a curse if an innocent man is slain and reparations are not made (see Deut. 21:1-9). With those words, these outspoken Pharisees pronounced, upon themselves and their children, a self- inflicted judgment based upon their law. Thus, the judgment for shedding innocent blood had to come within forty years in order to judge the two generations that imposed the curse upon themselves with the words, "His blood be upon us."

I believe the one trigger that releases the moment of judgment is when the cup of iniquity becomes full. The Lord informed Abraham of this and predicted that Abraham's seed would be out of the land, but after four hundred years, they would return to the land when the iniquity of the Amorites was full (Gen. 15:16). The imagery here is that of an empty cup that has something poured into it, until it becomes too full to hold the liquid and begins to overflow. The liquid representing unrepentant sins of the people pours into the cup continually, causing the cup to fill. Once the cup is full, there is no more room for iniquity and the overflow begins. The moment the cup is full and overflowing, judgment can be released. The overflowing cup indicates that the seasons of repentance have passed.

This same full cup principle is evident in the Apocalypse, when John saw the woman (representing Rome in his day) with a golden cup full of abominations and filthiness (Rev. 17:4). Mercy and grace can be extended to a half-full cup or a nearly full cup, but once the rim is full to the brim and overflowing, judgment comes. Even in the Book of Daniel, the prophet spoke of the rise of the Antichrist in the latter days, and noted that his appearance is linked to the time when the "transgressors are come to full" (Dan. 8:23).

DELAYED JUDGMENT IS NOT DENIED JUDGMENT

One often unobserved incident during the days of Noah illustrates how judgment can seem to be delayed, but it does not mean that judgment has been denied by God. Among the first ten generations from Adam to the flood, two older, righteous men were living at the same time the ark was being built: Noah and his great-great grandfather,

Methuselah. The year of the flood, Noah was 600 years of age and Methuselah was 969! Methuselah was the son of Enoch, the godly man who lived 365 years and was translated alive to heaven. Enoch was given insight and special revelations concerning the fallen angels, giants, heaven, and the future, according to numerous traditions handed down in a book called the Book of Enoch. Enoch walked with God and at age sixty-five Methuselah was born. Enoch was aware of a future judgment coming to the earth that would involve water, and he was given insight into the timing of the event, as revealed when we understand the Hebrew meaning of the name Methuselah. The name has two components: *muth*, a Hebrew word that means death, and *shalack*, which means to bring or to send forth. Thus his name can mean "his death will bring," and in the context and timing of his death, it refers to the global destruction by water!

One can go to Genesis chapters 5 – 7 and calculate the ages of Noah and Methuselah, and see that Methuselah died the same year that the flood erupted on the earth. Individuals in the ancient cultures understood the meaning of names, and in Noah's day men would have known that Methuselah's death would *initiate a judgment* on earth. This judgment of the world's destruction by water was revealed as far back as Adam. Josephus reports this amazing prediction passed down through Adam's seed:

> "They also were the inventors of that peculiar sort of wisdom which is concerned with the heavenly bodies and their order. And that their inventions might not be lost before they were sufficiently known, upon Adam's prediction that the world was to be destroyed at one time by the force of fire and another time by the violence and quantity of water, they made two pillars; the one of brick, and the other of stone: they inscribed their discoveries on them both, that in case the pillar of brick should be destroyed by the flood, the pillar of stone might remain, and exhibit those discoveries to mankind; and also inform them that there was another pillar of brick erected by them. Now this remains in the land of Siriad to this day."
>
> – JOSEPHUS; ANTIQUITIES OF THE JEWS, CHAPTER II, PART 3

Methuselah was the son of Enoch, and Enoch was translated, not seeing death (Gen. 5:21-24). The pre-flood men would have been aware of two things: the prediction of Adam indicating a global destruction by water, and the prophetic meaning of Methuselah's name. The water warning was etched in brick and stone, and could have been read by anyone. The second warning was concealed in one man's name. Today, a Bible is available for anyone to read, and the Holy Word clearly gives signs of both the coming of Christ and the Tribulation that follows.

In the flood narrative, the ark was prepared, the animals were in the ark, and God said, "Yet seven days I will cause it to rain upon the earth" (Gen. 7:4). Why would God have all things prepared, and yet wait seven days before sending the flood? An example of this delay is also found in the parable of the ten virgins. The ten virgins were all aware the bridegroom was coming and were anticipating his return; however, the bridegroom delayed his return. When the announcement came that he was coming for his bride, five virgins were unprepared.

God delayed the flood for seven days and Methuselah was the reason why. Notice that Methuselah was not in the ark; thus he died before the flood came. It is suggested by many scholars that the old patriarch did not pass away until everything related to the ark was *completely set in order*. When he passed in death, God gave Noah and his family seven additional days to bury Methuselah and to mourn for him. Biblically, there are different days set aside for mourning the deaths of noted patriarchs and leaders. The Egyptians mourned Jacob for seventy days (Gen. 50:3), Israel for Aaron thirty days (Num. 20:29), and Israel for Moses thirty days (Deut. 34:8). When Job was struck by a Satanic attack, for seven days he sat on the ground and said nothing as his grief was great (Job 2:13).

A Jewish mourning is known as shiva (meaning seven, because it last for seven days). Shiva is observed by family members of the deceased who usually meet at the home of the departed. Shiva begins on the day of the burial and continues until the morning of the seventh day. It appears that the Lord allowed Noah and his family the shiva to mourn the death of the oldest man to ever live before sending the flood at the conclusion of seven days.

SEVEN DAYS — WHAT DID PEOPLE THINK?

Here is the possible scenario related to the seven days from the completion of the ark to the day the rain began. When reading the narrative, I once assumed these seven days could have given an opportunity for a few individuals living near the ark to climb aboard and secure a place in the huge ship prior to the flood. I call this the "seven-day grace period." Prior to each judgment cycle, there is always a brief window to prepare for escape or to plan for the event. However, the people viewing the ark's construction (being from the lineage of Adam, and knowing the prophecy of the coming flood and the meaning of Methuselah's name) could expect the watery judgment the very day Methuselah died. But the day the patriarch passed away, no flood waters were released during the entire seven days. I can hear the voices of skeptics saying, "Well, the old man died and nothing happened!" Or, "What a fool Noah made of himself by building this ark!"

When Methuselah died, people would have expected something to happen immediately. But nobody knew of the seven days God had planned prior to the flood. It is that one *additional week* that may have given the skeptics a false sense of relief that the lad born to Enoch 969 years ago was not such a prophetic sign after all. At the conclusion of the seven days of Noah's mourning, however, the sky turned dark, lightning streaked across the heavens, and thunder rumbled over the earth. As the surface rocks and the plates under the earth cracked, the end had arrived for the Noah generation.

IT HAD NEVER RAINED BEFORE

It may have been difficult for Noah's generation to comprehend the idea of water covering the earth, as many believe that it had never rained before on the planet. This idea is based upon Moses' comment concerning the Garden of Eden.

According to the Genesis account, there was one main river that flowed through the Garden of Eden and parted into four divisions. From here flowed the four headwaters of the rivers Euphrates, Hiddekel (Tigris), Pishon, and Gihon (see Gen. 2:10-14). The Euphrates and Hiddekel are rivers that run from Armenia and Turkey, south into

Syria and Iraq, then becoming one river in Bozrah, eventually emptying into the Persian Gulf. The Pishon is believed to be a now non-existent river that once ran through Saudi Arabia. The Gihon, which passes through Egypt and empties into the Mediterranean Sea, is now called the Nile River according to Josephus.

Moses wrote the following:

> "This is the history of the heavens and the earth when they were created, in the day that the LORD God made the earth and the heavens, before any plant of the field was in the earth and before any herb of the field had grown. For the LORD God had not caused it to rain on the earth, and there was no man to till the ground; but a mist went up from the earth and watered the whole face of the ground."
>
> – GENESIS 2:4-6 (NKJV)

The Hebrew word for mist is *ed* and means a fog or a vapor. Early civilizations were built along rivers, and in the garden, moisture from a mist (watery vapor) provided the necessary water for every tree, plant and herb. This equal distribution of moisture guaranteed that all plants would be nourished and the garden would be lush and productive. There is an assumption that this was the method God used to water the earth prior to the flood. Because the upper and lower firmaments were created, others believe there were seasons of moderate rain, but not massive flooding.

Noah was given 100 to 120 years to build the ark (See Gen. 5:32; 6:3; 7:6). Assuming at that time the earth was only watered by early morning vapors, then for Noah to preach that destruction was coming by massive amounts of water would have seemed like a tall tale concocted by an overly imaginative old man. How can a person comprehend a warning when they have nothing with which to compare that warning? According to Josephus, God also warned Adam that the earth would at some point be destroyed by fire. This fire prediction is confirmed in two verses penned by the Apostle Peter. He wrote:

"But the heavens and the earth which are now preserved by the same word, are reserved for fire until the day of judgment and perdition of ungodly men."

— 2 PETER 3:7 (NKJV)

"But the day of the Lord will come as a thief in the night, in which the heavens will pass away with a great noise, and the elements will melt with fervent heat; both the earth and the works that are in it will be burned up."

— 2 PETER 3:10 (NKJV)

This destruction by fire has been explained a couple of possible ways. First, it could happen by a global nuclear war during the Tribulation, which would wreck the earth to a level unseen in world history. This theory is linked with the warning Christ gave, that unless those days (of the Tribulation) would be shortened, no flesh would be saved (Matt. 24:22). While the Tribulation will bring a record number of deaths and untold devastation, Peter spoke of the "day of judgment of ungodly men." This judgment is set in heaven and is identified as the great white throne judgment at the conclusion of Christ's thousand year reign (Rev. 20:11-15). Following this judgment, God will create a new heaven and a new earth (Rev. 21:1). To do this, the present heaven and earth must be dissolved, or as Peter indicated, set on fire.

One hundred years ago, if I said that entire cities and nations can be destroyed almost instantly by fire and heat, nobody could have comprehended that. However, with nuclear weapons this is now possible. A modern weapon, the nuclear bomb, can fulfill the vision of a sudden fireball of destruction. In Noah's day, the idea of water covering the planet and killing all life forms seemed more mythological than possible.

Here is the prophetic parallel. Biblically astute believers who understand the prophecies related to Christ's return are speaking of a soon catching away from Earth to heaven, in which true believers will be instantly changed from mortality to immortality. To the unbeliever who lacks faith and walks by sight, this concept is not only foolish but impossible. When *rationalizing* the resurrection, too many questions arise with too few answers. Perhaps this is why Paul called the resurrection a mystery (1 Cor. 15:51). The Greek word mystery is *musterion*, and refers to a silence imposed by being initiated into religious rites. Paul's use of this word was to say that the resurrection of the dead and the change occurring to those living at Christ's return could not be understood by natural reasoning, but only by divine revelation. In the normal sense, the Greek word mystery was something that could not be made known because the knowledge was being withheld. However, in the biblical sense, the word is used of the unknown being made known through divine revelation and knowledge of the Holy Spirit.

Prophetic ministers and those who believe in Christ's return are continually mocked as doom and gloom prognosticators who spread fear and anxiety. This reaction is especially true when declaring that Christ is returning soon. Doubters cannot imagine people rising off the planet and suddenly being zapped away to another galaxy. Yet, despite their verbal mocking, the Bible gives us four examples of people translated from Earth to heaven—two in human bodies and two in resurrected bodies:

- Enoch was translated alive to heaven in his physical body (Gen. 5:24; Heb. 11:5)

- Elijah was transported, in his physical body, to heaven in a chariot of fire (2 Kings 2:11)

- Jesus was lifted into heaven in His glorified body (Acts 1:9)

- The saints who came out of the grave after Christ's resurrection were taken to heaven at some point (Matt. 27:52-53)

The Bible teaches that, even if some do not believe, their unbelief cannot prevent the Word of God from being true (see Rom. 3:3-4). The skepticism of Lot's sons-in-law to Lot's warning did not hinder the judgment from striking Sodom the following morning (Gen. 19:14). Likewise, the unbelief of multitudes did not restrain the floodwaters from swallowing sinners in the flood. The unbelief of Joseph's brothers toward his dreams did not prevent Joseph from fulfilling his destiny. The unbelief in Christ's day may have hindered miracles, such as in Nazareth (Matt. 13:54-58), but the unbelief of many Pharisees could not prevent God's purpose in Christ from being fulfilled at the cross and the resurrection. Neither will the world's unbelief hinder the return of the Messiah.

CHAPTER 3

WHO CAN ESCAPE
WHAT IS COMING?

A LARGE NUMBER OF believers are familiar with the prophetic teaching of the Antichrist, the final kingdom of the beast, and the Great Tribulation. Scholars, however, have opposing viewpoints, not concerning interpretation of the symbolism found in apocalyptic literature (Daniel and Revelation), as much as they are related to the timing and order of certain events.

The deepest rift among prophetic students deals with the *timing* of the coming of Christ for the living saints and the resurrected dead in Christ (1 Thess. 4:16-17; 1 Cor. 15:51-54). There are three primary opinions about the timing of this event—before the Tribulation, in the middle of the Tribulation, and at the end of the seven-year Tribulation. Most biblically literate evangelicals acknowledge a future seven-year Tribulation in which one man, identified as the Antichrist, will unite a final eighth kingdom of ten nations during the last half of the Tribulation and rule for forty-two months (Dan. 9:27; Rev. 17:11-12; Rev. 11:2).

Millions believe in the *catching away* or the *gathering together*—biblical terms used to identify what some call the "rapture". The question is: Where is the rapture in relation to the events and judgments that occur during the Tribulation?

Those who believe the catching away occurs at the beginning of the seven-year Tribulation call their theory the pre-Tribulation return of Christ. If the event occurs before the Tribulation, the church will *escape* the apocalyptic judgments recorded from Revelation chapter 5 through 18.

Those who believe in a mid-Tribulation return place the event at Revelation chapter 11—about the middle point of the Tribulation. They believe the church will be on Earth through the first forty-two months of the Tribulation and experience the judgments of the wrath of God that are released during that time period. They believe that the return of Christ occurs at some point when the "mystery of God is finished," at the time the seventh angel of the apocalypse appears in heaven (Rev. 10:7).

The third view, called the post-Tribulation appearing of Christ, places the church on Earth during the entire seven years of Tribulation and teaches that many Christians will be martyred having to choose between accepting or rejecting the mark of the beast (Rev. 13:18). In this view, Christ returns at the end of the seven years with the armies of heaven to defeat the Antichrist and his armies (see Revelation 19). Some teach we will be changed when Christ appears, and the dead in Christ will be raised. We will ascend into the clouds, then come back to Earth.

Those who place Christ's return before or at the beginning of the Tribulation have several reasons for believing this. First, they understand the purpose for this terrible time of trouble in world history. The Old Testament prophets saw this time and called it *the day of God's vengeance*, and the *time of Jacob's trouble*—Jacob meaning Israel (Isa. 61:2; Jer. 30:7). At different junctures in his writings, Daniel unlocks one reason for the coming Tribulation, and it involves Israel.

Remember that Daniel was written by a Jew to Jews and for Israel in the future. When he described the final beast's kingdom, he said that this beast would make war with the saints (Dan. 7:21) and would wear out the saints of the most High (Dan. 7:25). In a second vision, Daniel was told that in the latter time a ruler would come who would destroy the mighty and the holy people (Dan. 8:24). In the closing section of Daniel, an angel of the Lord made this statement: "...and when he shall have accomplished to scatter the power of the holy people, all of these things shall be finished" (Dan. 12:7). Daniel made it clear that the holy people and the saints were his people—the Jews—who would experience another time of great distress in the future. .

In the book of Revelation, the dragon (Satan) and the Antichrist (the beast) are united for the destruction of Israel. One entire chapter in Revelation was penned on the heavenly battle over the man-child and the woman, with the woman symbolizing national Israel. Satan does all in his power to persecute the woman, and eventually sends a flood to her hiding place in the wilderness in hopes of eradicating this remnant seed of Israel from the earth (see Revelation chapter 12). This chapter concludes by saying, "The dragon was wroth [angry] with the woman, and went to make war with the remnant of her seed" (Rev. 12:17).

The Hebrew prophets clearly identified this time as the end of the age when national Israel will be under siege by the Antichrist, his armies and Satan, whose failed attempt to destroy the Jewish people will climax with Satan himself experiencing his own confinement in the abyss (Rev. 20:1-2).

Jacob worked seven years for his wife Rachel and received the wrong one, then had to work seven more years to get the one he was promised (Gen. 29:20-28). Prophetically, Jacob's trouble is Israel's final seven years, which will conclude with the appearing of their true, anticipated Messiah (Dan. 9:27).

From God's viewpoint, the Tribulation is also a time of His wrath being released upon sinners. Isaiah said God would destroy sinners off the earth during this time (see Isaiah 13:9). In John's apocalyptic vision, he saw strange cosmic judgments in the sun and stars that impacted Earth—including a massive asteroid, falling stars, and the darkening of the sun (see Revelation 6:12-14). Other judgments include famines, droughts, earthquakes and volcanic eruptions. The Earth and even the entire cosmos will experience severe troubles that will impact those who are living on Earth when these events begin.

The purpose of the Tribulation is threefold: to lead the Jewish remnant to repentance and acceptance of Christ their Messiah; to purge the Earth of sinners and ungodly wicked nations; and to bring an end to Satan's dominion by manifesting the visible Kingdom of God that will be ruled by Christ the King.

DO BELIEVERS ESCAPE OR ENDURE?

Are true believers who are in covenant with Christ marked for a great *escape* from the Tribulation, or should we prepare for a long-term *endurance* test? It was Jesus who said, "He that shall endure unto the end, the same shall be saved" (Matt. 24:13). All believers must endure hardships, persecution, and trials throughout their lives. However, for those whose theological stance is centered on a pre-Tribulation return of Christ for the church, numerous Scriptures support their stance.

The first observation is that the future Tribulation is identified as the "wrath of the Lamb" and the "wrath of God" (Rev. 6:16; 14:10). The Greek word for *wrath* of the Lamb in Revelation 6:16 is *orge* which means *anger, indignation, vengeance.* The *wrath* of God in 14:10 uses a different Greek word *thumos,* and this word is connected to a more fierce anger, such as when a person is so angry they begin breathing hard. This second word is used in Revelation 14:8, 10; 15:1, 7; 16:19, all of which are verses dealing with the second half of the Tribulation. These references in the Apocalypse indicate God's wrath being poured out from vials, using a metaphor of the cup of the fierceness of His wrath (Rev. 16:19). God has His own heavenly cup that becomes full; and once full, the explosive cosmic and earthly judgments are unleashed.

In Matthew 3:7, "fleeing the wrath to come" might have had reference to the future destruction of Jerusalem that Christ alluded to in Luke 21:23. Christ spoke of that time as distress on the land with wrath upon the people. However, there is also a future wrath that can and must be avoided. Those who refuse to believe and who reject Christ's redemptive covenant are abiding under the wrath of God (John 3:36).

In the epistles, more insight is gleaned regarding God's wrath on the sinner. When people harden their hearts, they are storing up wrath for the day of God's wrath and righteous judgment (see Rom. 2:5). Paul warned that indignation and wrath, including tribulation and anguish to every soul, await those who obey not the truth (Rom. 2:8-9). In Ephesians 5, Paul listed numerous sins that saints are to avoid, and he added this statement, "for because of these things cometh the wrath of God upon the children of disobedience" (Eph. 5:6). In numerous verses of Scripture, the wrath of God is not released upon any believer who follows Christ and is saved through His blood. It is unleashed over time against the sinners, the unrepentant, and the ungodly.

The New Testament indicates there is protection from the wrath to come for those in covenant with Christ. When we are justified (made just and righteous) by the blood of Christ, we shall be saved from wrath through Him (Rom. 5:9). Paul's first epistle was a letter known as First Thessalonians. In it he mentions the coming of the Lord and the revelation of our gathering together unto Christ (1 Thess. 4:16-17). He encourages believers with these words: "For God hath not appointed us to wrath, but to obtain salvation by our Lord Jesus Christ" (1 Thess. 5:9). Paul also told this church that Jesus "delivered us from the wrath to come" (1 Thess. 1:10).

In Luke 21, Christ gave numerous signs of His coming, including the strange cosmic activity that would occur prior to His appearing on Earth. He gave this dynamic prayer that His followers should pray:

> "Watch ye therefore, and pray always, that ye may be accounted worthy to escape all of these things that shall come to pass, and to stand before the Son of man."
>
> – LUKE 21:36 (KJV)

In the context, escaping these things refers to believers who would be caught unaware at Christ's return, as they were bound up with drunkenness and the cares of daily living. Christ taught that these activities would be snares that would come upon the entire world (see Luke 21:34-36). God's will is that Christ's true disciples escape these things. However, if we read the verses prior to verse 36, Christ revealed there would be frightening cosmic activity during the Tribulation, and that God's judgment (days of vengeance – v. 22) will be discharged on the earth. Praying to be accounted worthy to escape all these things refers to the whole of the subject—the snares prior to His return, and the horrific events of the Tribulation that will cause men's hearts to fail them for fear (Luke 21:22-26).

The Greek word for escape in Luke 21:36 is *ekpheugo*, meaning *to flee out of.* The same Greek word is used in Acts 16:27 of the escape of prisoners; in Acts 19:16 of the seven sons of Sceva fleeing from the demon possessed man; and in 2 Corinthians 11:33 of Paul escaping from Damascus. To escape is to remove oneself from one location to another. Notice after fleeing, we will "stand before the son of man." This seems to allude to the Judgment Seat of Christ that is prepared for all believers in heaven. John mentioned this in Revelation:

> "The nations were angry, and Your wrath has come,
> And the time of the dead, that they should be judged,
> And that You should reward Your servants the prophets and the saints,
> And those who fear Your name, small and great,
> And should destroy those who destroy the earth."
>
> – Rev. 11:18 (NKJV)

Here are the principles of the wrath of God:

1. God reserves His wrath for His enemies (Nahum 1:2)

2. God's wrath is for the disobedient and not for the obedient (Rom. 2:8-9)

3. God provides a way of escape for the righteous prior to wrath being unleashed (2 Pet. 2:9)

THE ESCAPE METHODS

Many years before the Babylonian invasion of Jerusalem, God forewarned Judah that they were provoking Him with their iniquities. At times Israel was so far away from God, they were offering their children to false gods, permitting Sodomites to live just outside the temple, breaking the Sabbath, and not keeping the sacred festivals. As their cup became full, God's anger became heated and the true prophets warned the people of God's wrath being poured out (Jer. 50:13; Ezek. 13:15; Hos. 13:11).

When wrath is being unleashed, there is still a spiritual principle of separating the sheep from goats, wheat from tares, good from bad, light from darkness, the righteous from the unrighteous. This separation was evident in Moses' time in Egypt. Plagues were unleashed on the Egyptians, causing damage to crops, pollution to rivers, and havoc on Egypt's economy. However, God placed a separation—an invisible barrier—between the Egyptians and the Hebrews. The plagues never impacted any Hebrew home, cattle or property, as God set a boundary between His people and their people (Exod. 9:4). Moses wrote:

> "And I will sever in that day the land of Goshen, in which my people dwell, that no swarms of flies shall be there; to the end thou mayest know that I am the LORD in the midst of the earth. And I will put a division between my people and thy people; tomorrow shall this sign be."
>
> – EXODUS 8:22-23 (KJV)

The process of righteous men and women escaping the wrath of God is as follows. The first method is for a believer to be warned in advance, thus providing time to sell their possessions and move to a different location. In Acts, believers in Jerusalem sold their possessions to assist poor believers (Acts 4:36-37; 5:1). This was done for several reasons. First, the church was growing rapidly and widows needed food and financial support; thus these sales provided for the distribution of income and goods for their needs. Second, Christ had predicted that Jerusalem would be destroyed within one generation (Matt. 23:34-38; 24:1-3). Knowing the sacred city had a limited time before destruction, believers knew the buildings would be in ruins; thus believers set out early to sell property with many relocating to other areas, years before the destruction came.

The second form of escape is revealed in the narrative of Lot. There were five cities on the southern end of the Dead Sea. When destructive fire suddenly struck, four of the five cities were in ashes with a total loss of life, with the exception of Lot and his two daughters who found refuge on a mountain near a very small town called Zoar. It is difficult to explain how four cities were in the blast zone, but one in the same region went untouched. The answer is found in the comments of the two angels. These two heavenly messengers were assigned to destroy all five cities. However, since Lot chose Zoar, the angels set a hedge of protection around the town where Lot would dwell, thus exempting it from being consumed by fire (see Genesis 19:17-22). Zoar's protection was supernatural; it was not some natural phenomenon.

Lot's escape to a mountain runs parallel with a statement in Revelation, where in the first half of the Tribulation men will run to the mountains and caves, wishing the rocks would fall upon them (see Revelation 6:15). I live close to the famous Smokey Mountains in Tennessee. On these beautiful mountains, people have erected log homes that overlook the lush green valleys or the crystal clear rivers. People often feel more secure, being away from large crowds and the high crime areas of America's cities. Thus, escaping can include relocating from a large city to a smaller and safer community, where people watch out for each other, and perhaps farm their land and dig wells for water.

Both Noah and the prophets Ezekiel and Jeremiah demonstrate another view of escaping judgment, which is for individuals to be preserved in the midst of destruction all around them. As the flood waters lifted the Ark above the mountains, Noah and his family rode out the flood that covered the earth for over one year. Prior to the Babylonian invasion and captivity, Ezekiel saw a vision of angels with inkhorns, commissioned to mark the foreheads of those who were grieved over the abominations being committed in Jerusalem. The angel said multitudes would be slain in the city; however, any man with the invisible mark of God on their foreheads would be spared from the destruction (Ezek. 9:1-6). The reasons for the destruction were that the land was full of innocent blood, and the city was full of perverseness (Ezek. 9:9).

Following the siege and burning of Jerusalem and the temple by the Babylonians, the Jewish survivors were chained and assembled for a long, treacherous journey across the mountains and deserts to Babylon.

Jeremiah was marked for captivity, but he was recognized by a captain of the guards and given a choice to stay in the land of Israel or go to Babylon. He was released and remained in Israel with a small remnant (see Jeremiah 39 and 40).

Throughout biblical history, God has always had a righteous remnant to whom He gave a plan of escape or provided a way of protection. The same is true during the Tribulation when 144,000 Jewish men are sealed with the seal of God and protected from the judgments of God and the Antichrist (Rev. 7 and 14:1). Perhaps Peter summed it up best when—speaking of Lot being warned in advance and his escape from Sodom—he wrote, "For the Lord knows how to deliver the godly..." (2 Pet. 2:9).

For the believer, is the future *escape* or *endurance*? The answer is both. The Christian life in general requires us, at times, to endure hardness and persecution (2 Tim. 2:3; 3:12). One of the promises of God for escaping temptation reads:

> "No temptation has overtaken you except such as is common to man; but God is faithful, who will not allow you to be tempted beyond what you are able, but with the temptation will also make the way of escape, that you may be able to bear it."
>
> – 1 CORINTHIANS 10:13 (NKJV)

The spiritual principle throughout the Bible is that God makes avenues of escape for those who trust in His covenant. Israel escaped a famine in the days of Joseph (Gen. 47). Abraham was given a plan of escape, to sojourn in Egypt at the time a severe famine was striking the Promised Land (Gen. 12:10). Jeremiah warned Israel for centuries that the Babylonians would invade Judea, seize Jerusalem, destroy the city, and take the people into captivity for seventy years (Jer. 25:11). Prior to the Babylonian invasion of Judea, angels with inkhorns marked the foreheads of the righteous who were crying out against the sins of the nation. The word "mark" used to describe the invisible symbol placed on the heads of the righteous is the word *tav* in Hebrew. Each Hebrew letter has a specific symbol it represents. The symbol of the tav is a cross—either † or X. Thus the emblem of the cross was the mark that set apart the righteous who would be spared during the invasion.

When Christ was in deep intercession before becoming the sin offering for mankind, God had provided a way of escape if Christ chose not to follow through with God's plan from the foundation of the world. Christ confessed that God could send twelve legions of angels (about 72,000) to intervene in the process. However, Christ drank from the cup of sufferings and fulfilled the plan of redemption (Matt. 26:53-54).

Christ gave the signs of the end of the age and the dangerous cosmic activity that will be released during the Tribulation. He then made the following statement to His followers:

> "Watch ye therefore, and pray always, that ye may be accounted worthy to escape all these things that shall come to pass, and to stand before the Son of Man."
>
> – LUKE 21:36 (KJV)

In 1 Thessalonians 5:5, Paul spoke of those who walk in the truth (light), and those who walk in darkness. He addressed the unbelievers as "they," and warned they would not escape the destruction coming (1 Thess. 5:3). He reminded the believers that they are not in darkness, that the future would overtake them. He instructed them to remain alert and sober, and to put on faith. He concluded with this important statement: "For God has not appointed us to wrath, but to obtain salvation by our Lord Jesus Christ (1 Thess. 5:5-9).

Christ bore our sins at the cross, and thus carried any wrath assigned to us. Because He suffered in our place, we are not appointed to the wrath of God's judgment if we walk in repentance and remain under the covering of the blood of Christ. The one verse that sums up God's escape from wrath for those in covenant with Him is:

> "And to wait for his Son from heaven, whom he raised from the dead, even Jesus, which delivered us from the wrath to come."
>
> – 1 THESS. 1:10 (KJV)

CHAPTER 4

THE MYSTERY OF THE
MISSING 70 YEARS

S EVERAL YEARS AGO, when reading of the Fall of Adam and a
warning God gave him, I was perplexed as to why the warning
did not seem to be completely fulfilled. Normally when
exploring this type of biblical "contradiction," there is actually a deeper
meaning—called a *prophetic layer*—that is concealed within the narrative that must be searched out for clarity.

When God created Adam, he was formed as a mature adult. The
Scripture does not answer several questions, such as: How old did
Adam look? Rabbinical sources imply he appeared twenty to thirty, as
twenty in the Torah was the age that a young man went to war, and
thirty was the time a young man could enter the priesthood (Num.
1:3; 4:3). We also are not told how long Adam lived sin-free in the
Garden of Eden. We know he named all of the animals (which seem-
ingly would have consumed much time), and we know Eve was created
and they were told to be fruitful and multiply (Gen. 1:28). We sometimes assume from the biblical narrative that Adam was formed from
the dust, Eve was formed from his rib, and within just a few days, they
sinned.

While the biblical record is silent, the book of Jubilees, written
in the second century BC, records that Adam and Eve lived in the
garden for seven years. In a footnote in the works of Josephus, who
lived prior to and after the destruction of the temple, the historian

wrote: "The number of Adam's children, as says the old tradition, was thirty-three sons and twenty-three daughters." Again, we assume that children must have been born in the garden, since Cain—the first son born after the Fall—went to the land of Nod and married a wife, which was years after Adam was expelled. The wife of Cain likely would have been a sister, which was something forbidden (physical relations with a sister) later in the Torah. The second point is, after being expelled from the garden, God told Eve, "I will greatly multiply thy sorrow and thy conception; in sorrow [meaning physical pain] thou shalt bring forth children…" (Gen. 3:16). The logical reasoning is that Eve must have experienced childbirth without any pains before being cast out of God's presence, and now is being warned that pain will accompany all future births.

There were two distinct trees in Eden, whose fruit would be like the two sides of a magnet—one positive and the other negative. One tree would sustain spiritual and physical life, and the other would initiate spiritual and physical death. God said that Adam could eat from every tree in the garden, except the tree of the knowledge of good and evil, warning that "in the day you eat thereof you will surely die" (Gen. 2:17). Herein lies the mystery.

Both Adam and Eve ate from the tree of knowledge of good and evil. When they did, their eyes were opened to understand the impact of sin, disobedience and evil. Yet, neither Adam nor Eve died physically at that moment. This death was first spiritual—a separation from God's presence—followed hundreds of years later by their physical deaths. In fact, when Adam was expelled from the garden, he and Eve were blessed with two sons—Cain and Abel. But Cain slew Abel and fled from his parents. Adam was well over 120 years of age when this occurred; thus the earth had been populated by the Adam's seed for many years.

Adam was 130 years of age when Abel's replacement, Seth, was born. Beginning with Seth, God raised up nine righteous men in succession: Seth, Enos, Cainan, Mahalaleel, Jared, Enoch, Methuselah, Lamech, and Noah (see Genesis 5:1-32).

Adam was warned that in the day he ate from the tree, he would die. The Hebrew word here for day is *yom*, the common word for a literal twenty-four-hour day. We could assume that Adam should have died, both *spiritually* and *physically*, the same day he bit into the fruit. However, Adam lived a very long life of 930 years (see Genesis 5:5). The question then becomes, was God referring to something deeper when He said, "In the day you eat, you will die"?

To answer this, we look to the fact that all men, prior to the flood, lived long lives. Moses noted the pre-flood lifespans of the first ten generations:

- Adam lived 930 years (Gen. 5:5)
- Seth lived 912 years (Gen 5:8)
- Enos lived 905 years (Gen. 5:11)
- Cainan lived 910 years (Gen. 5:14)
- Mahalaleel lived 895 years (Gen. 5:17)
- Jared lived 962 years (Gen. 5:20)
- Enoch lived 365 years (Gen. 5:23)
- Methuselah lived 969 years (Gen. 5:27)
- Lamech lived 777 years (Gen. 5:31)
- Noah lived 950 years (Gen. 9:29)

Notice that seven of the ten men from Adam to Noah lived over 900 years.

THE THOUSAND-YEAR DAY

The solar day is twenty-four hours (in which the earth spins one complete rotation) and the solar year is 365 days (in which the earth completely circles the sun). However, two times the Bible reveals how God views time from a different perspective. We read:

"For a thousand years in thy sight are but as yesterday when it is past, and as a watch in the night."

> — PSALMS 90:4 (KJV)

"But, beloved, be not ignorant of this one thing, that one day is with the Lord as a thousand years, and a thousand years as one day."

> — 2 PETER 3:8 (KJV)

In God's realm, time as we know it here on earth does not exist. He lives in timelessness—also called eternity. Time became important at the Fall of Adam, yet time will cease at the conclusion of the great white throne judgment, which is an event that will occur in the ages to come (Eph. 2:7). Then, the saints of God will enter the *no time zone*.

Pre-flood men lived long lives, some over nine hundred years, but they all fell short of one thousand years. To God, one day was a thousand years (2 Peter 3:8). Thus, in the *day* that Adam ate of the tree, he died. His physical death occurred at age 930, which is seventy years short of completing a one-thousand-year "day of the Lord."

To demonstrate how a thousand years represents one prophetic day, when Christ (the last Adam, see 1 Cor. 15:45) returns to Earth at the conclusion of a seven-year Tribulation, He will set up His global government which will rule all nations for one thousand years. According to Revelation 20, the following occurs:

- Satan is taken from the earth and bound in the abyss for a thousand years (Rev. 20:2-3)

- All saints, including Tribulation martyrs, will rule with Christ for a thousand years (Rev. 20:4)

- After the thousand years, Satan is loosed for a season to test men and attack Jerusalem (Rev. 20:7-8)

- Satan will be cast into the lake of fire and a great judgment will occur in heaven (Rev. 20:11-12)

- At the end of the thousand years and after this judgment, heaven and earth will be renovated (Rev. 21:1)

Why does Christ rule a thousand years, and not one hundred, five hundred, or several thousand? The principle is in the phrase, *the day of the Lord*, which is found in both the Old and New Testaments, and seems to have different implications depending on the context of the verse. At times the phrase refers to invading armies fighting over Jerusalem or in Judea, and causing great suffering and anguish for the Jewish people. The phrase is first used by Isaiah, and later incorporated in both prophetic and apocalyptic predictions related to both Israel and the nations. Isaiah indicated cosmic disturbances would impact inhabitants on Earth during the day of the Lord (see Isaiah 13).

In the apocalyptic context, Joel speaks of the cosmic harbingers occurring "before the great and terrible day of the Lord" (Joel 2:31). In the New Testament, the phrase or similar phrases are used in connection with the judgments released during the future Great Tribulation.

Much could be written concerning "the day of the Lord." However, if we sum up the various meanings, they are:

- The set time when invading armies would attack Israel, Judea and Jerusalem

- The set time in the Tribulation when numerous judgments are unleashed in heaven and on Earth

- The day the Tribulation concludes, initiating the first day of Christ's reign on Earth

- The thousand years when Christ is ruling from Jerusalem over the nations

These events occur over a period of years and not one twenty-four-hour day. When we focus on the concept that the "day of the Lord" can also allude to a thousand years, then prophetically the Messiah will restore the earth and the animal kingdom to a pre-Fall status, as it relates to spiritual dominion. Adam fell short of a perfect day by seventy years, but the Messiah will complete the "day" cycle. Through Adam, God's day was disrupted by sin and death; however, through Christ, the last Adam, the one-thousand-year day of the Lord will be a complete cycle of global peace and prosperity, as men will beat their swords into plowshares (Joel 3:10), as the wolf and the lamb will lie together, and children can play near formerly poisonous serpents and not fear (Isa. 11:6-8).

SEVENTY YEARS SHORT

Had Adam not disobeyed God's instruction, he would have lived to be a thousand and beyond, as death entered the world because of sin (Rom. 5:12). He died within a "day" on God's prophetic calendar. Note that Adam was seventy years short of a thousand years. Seventy is a significant number among the Jewish people and is found in the Bible sixty-one times in sixty verses. It first appears in the story of Cain's descendent Lamech, who slew a man. Lamech said, "If Cain shall be avenged sevenfold, truly Lamech seventy and sevenfold" (Gen. 4:24).

Seventy here is first linked to punishment. Seventy multiplied seven times is 490, and Lamech stated this would be his punishment. This number is also prophetically important as it relates to Daniel's seventy weeks (see Daniel 9), which is seventy times seven of years, or 490 years, following the Babylonian captivity and the decree to rebuild the walls of Jerusalem, to the time when everlasting righteousness will come.

What is the significance of the number seventy? From the time when Adam was expelled from the garden to the time of his physical death is 70 years short of a thousand. Seventy becomes a significant number:

Exodus 1:5	Seventy souls came from the loins of Jacob
Numbers 11:16	Seventy elders were gathered to Moses from among the people
Isaiah 23:15	The city of Tyre would be forgotten for seventy years
Jeremiah 25:11	Israel would go into Babylonian captivity for seventy years
Luke 10:1	Christ appointed seventy to heal the sick and expel demons

According to Jewish rabbis, the number seventy is like a double-sided coin. On one hand it refers to complete unity, and on the other hand it represents disunity and confusion. Seventy souls came out of the loins of Jacob (Exod. 1:5). However, in Hebrew the word is a singular soul and not plural, indicating that the seventy men were in such unity. It was as though they were one man. According to Scripture, Jewish history, and commentary, Nimrod constructed a high building called the Tower of Babel. They credited their ability to unite under one language for the building's construction, thus their unity. However, when God saw their pride, He overthrew their tower, scattered the people across the earth, and divided the languages among seventy different tongues. Thus disunity in the world also took on the number seventy.

The Bible indicates there are three important numbers linked with seven. The first is the Sabbath which occurs every seventh day (originally, Saturday was the seventh day, or the Sabbath). The day marks a day of rest for animals and people. The next cycle is every seventh year, which is a Sabbatical year. The nation was not supposed to plant or harvest any crops or fruit trees on the Sabbatical year. The third cycle is the seven times seven or forty-nine year count, which introduced a cessation from all labor and released people from their debts, allowing them permission to have their lost family land inheritances restored. This cycle of every fifty years was called a Jubilee (see Leviticus 25).

These cycles were so important to God that He selected the time frame of seventy years for Israel's Babylonian captivity, because they had not kept the Jubilee cycle and allowed the land to rest (see 2 Chron. 34). Seventy can be a combination of the number ten multiplied seven times. Israel was given Ten Commandment to follow. The Almighty warned in the Torah that if they did not follow His Commandments and law, the people would see their punishment multiplied by seven (see Leviticus 26:18, 21, 28).

70 Short and 70 Final

Was it just a coincidence that Adam fell short of a prophetic day (that is, a thousand years), or is there a deeper implication in this? The seventy years is interesting, as this number appears when Israel was carried into Babylonian captivity for seventy years (Jer. 25:11). We then see the number appear again when the Jews were in their seventy years of captivity in Babylon, and Gabriel revealed that another seventy "weeks" was planned in connection with the completion of Israel's prophetic cycles. Daniel 9:24-27 provides a detailed description of the seventy weeks:

> "Seventy weeks [of years, or 490 years] have been decreed for your people and for your holy city [Jerusalem], to finish the transgression, to make an end of sins, to make atonement (reconciliation) for wickedness, to bring in everlasting righteousness [right-standing with God], to seal up vision and prophecy and prophet, and to anoint the Most Holy Place.

> "So you are to know and understand that from the issuance of the command to restore and rebuild Jerusalem until [the coming of] the Messiah (the Anointed One), the Prince, there will be seven weeks [of years] and sixty-two weeks [of years]; it will be built again, with [a city] plaza and moat, even in times of trouble.

> "Then after the sixty-two weeks [of years] the Anointed One will be cut off [and denied His Messianic kingdom] and have nothing [and no one to defend Him], and the people of the [other] prince who is to come will destroy the city and the sanctuary. Its end will come with a flood; even to the end there will be war; desolations are determined.

> "And he will enter into a binding and irrevocable covenant with the many for one week [seven years], but in the middle of the week he will stop the sacrifice and grain offering [for the remaining three and one-half years]; and on the wing of abominations will come one who makes desolate, even until the complete destruction, one that is decreed, is poured out on the one who causes the horror."

> – Dan. 9:24-27 (AMP)

In the context of this passage, Daniel was studying the scroll of Jeremiah, where the prophet predicted Israel's seventy years of captivity. As this time was coming to a conclusion, Daniel was questioning God's future plans when the angel of God revealed that another future "seventy" was planned; this time not seventy years, but seventy times seven of years, or 490 years. The final seven years introduces the time of Great Tribulation and the rise of the Antichrist, and concludes with the visible return of Christ.

The last day of the Great Tribulation will also be the first day of the one-thousand-year reign of Christ. This is the culmination of the "day of the Lord." One day evil climaxes on Earth, and on the same day righteousness begins to rule. This explains why, in the Old Testament, the day of the Lord passages sometimes expose horrible judgment, and other times show a positive light on that day. This is the one day when the world is almost annihilated, yet it is also the one day when the Messiah rescues humanity from complete destruction.

A second explanation on the positive verses is regarding the reign of Christ on Earth, from Jerusalem, for one thousand years. This is a timeframe that, according to Peter, is "one day with the Lord." Adam's death was seventy years short of a thousand, and that time period must be completed to initiate the final day of the Lord that, once and for all, will defeat death and bring life through the last Adam.

I have called the one-thousand-year reign of Christ "the perfect day." Early Church Fathers noted that in the Genesis narrative, creation was completed in six days, and on the seventh day, God rested (Gen 2:2). Exchanging each day of creation for a thousand years, a theory emerged that said man's government would continue for six days, or six thousand years, with the seventh day being the one-thousand-year reign of Christ (Rev. 20:4). Thus, the world as we know it would experience a seven-thousand-year cycle that concludes with the great white throne judgment and the creation of a new heaven and earth (Rev. 21). In the Jewish Talmud is written, "The world is to exist six thousand years. In the first two thousand there was desolation; two thousand years the Torah flourished; and the next two thousand the Messianic era (Babylonian Talmud: Tractate Sanhedrin Folio 97a).

Thousands of years after the creation narrative, God led Israel out of the slavery of Egypt, where the Hebrews had worked non-stop without a day off, building treasure houses for Pharaoh. God initiated a law of Sabbath rest every seventh day for both man and beast.

Sabbath is believed to come from the root word *sabat*, which means to stop, cease and keep, or cease from work (Ex. 20:8-11; Deut. 5:12-15). The law was based upon the fact that God stopped creating on the sixth day and rested on the seventh. Thus the seventh day became holy, set apart, for Israel to enjoy a break from the travails of life. Even animals were given a break from working the fields.

This principle of the seventh day rest does, I believe, apply to the one-thousand-year reign of Christ. This Day of the Lord is the Earth's day of rest. There will be no wars during the thousand years, as men will beat their swords in plowshares and study war no more (Isa. 2:4). The natural strife between animals will cease, as "The wolf also shall dwell with the lamb, the leopard shall lie down with the young goat, the calf and the young lion and the fatling together; and a little child shall lead them" (Isa. 11:6). The changes during the Messiah's rule on the earth are so dramatic that a child can put his hand in a viper's den and not be harmed (Isa. 11:8).

When I read the numerous prophetic passages about Christ's rule on Earth, the dramatic changes to the hearts of people, the changes in the animal kingdom and so on, I compare the future to the beginning of creation. In the Garden of Eden, Adam had the rivers, trees, and animals; he had no war, murder or conflict until sin altered history and humanity. His perfect one-thousand-year day was cut short by seventy years. Christ, who is the last Adam, will rule from an Eden-like world for a thousand years, thus completing the perfect day that the first Adam failed to fulfill.

CHAPTER 5

KING SAUL: THE PATTERN
OF THE UNITED STATES

THE BIBLE IS the original book that reveals the ancient history of mankind and the early rise of Israel and the Jews. Since the history of the world is cyclical, there are many prophetic layers and prophetic patterns concealed in ancient narratives that can be repeated in the future—including in our time. Solomon understood this when he wrote: "That which has been is what will be, That which is done is what will be done, And there is nothing new under the sun" (Eccl. 1:9-10).

America is not directly found in biblical prophecy, despite numerous attempts to find it there by stretching Scriptures beyond their actual meaning. However, God conceals truth in parables, patterns, types and shadows, and repetitive historical cycles. In my book, *Nightmare Along Pennsylvania Avenue,* I showed some of those patterns. Politically, America's judicial and legislative patterns mirror those of the ancient Roman Empire. From a spiritual perspective, America and Israel are connected with numerous prophetic parallels.

Since Israel became a nation in 1948, each American president has found it necessary to deal with Israel, Jerusalem, or the Jewish people. In 1948, after assisting the Jewish people in receiving recognition of Israel at the United Nations, President Truman was overheard comparing himself to Cyrus, the Persian king who assisted the Jews in returning to Judea and rebuilding. In 1973, during Israel's

Yom Kippur War, without America's assistance Israel would have suffered greatly and perhaps lost part of their biblical land grant. Prime Minister Golda Meir called President Nixon at three o'clock in the morning, asking for needed military equipment. Nixon, upon hearing her plea, recalled his Quaker mother's voice and responded to Golda's request, allowing America to assist Israel in turning the war against her enemies. During the Carter administration, there was a major peace agreement between Israel and Egypt that continues to this day. Reagan made history by assisting in the fall of communism in the Soviet Union, and during the conclusion of his eighth year, Soviet Jews were given visas allowing their departure and return to Israel.

An unusual pattern emerged with the 41st President, Herbert Walker Bush, as he fought Saddam Hussein in Iraq. The war with Iraq, the land of ancient Babylon, correlates with 1 Kings 20:17-29.

In 1991 Saddam, who once called himself the "king of Babylon," invaded Kuwait. The international community feared he would move troops into other countries and seize valuable oil fields. When President Bush went to war, some parallels with that ancient biblical war in 1 Kings were seen:

The Old Testament War	The First Gulf War
32 kings with Ben-Hadad	32 nations in our coalition
Young men went to battle	Many soldiers were young men
Told to keep the enemy alive	We kept Iraqi troops alive
They fought in the plains	The coalition fought in the plains (deserts)
The enemy was in sackcloth & ropes, then released	We captured, then released them
Israel slew 100,000 men	About 100,000 Iraqis were killed
Israel made a treaty with the king to restore him	The coalition made agreements with Saddam
Ben-Hadad had a second war	America fought a second Iraqi war

One of the strangest prophetic parallels involved President Bill Clinton, who announced in 1992 that America would get "two for one," meaning his wife Hillary would also lead behind the scenes. The pattern of their administration fit well with an Old Testament couple, Ahab and Jezebel, found in 1 Kings chapters 16-22.

The Ahab and Jezebel History	The Clinton Parallels
He was the leader, yet she directed events	Bill was president, but Hillary directed events
The couple lived in an ivory house	The president lives in the White House
The couple was involved in a land deal	The Clintons were involved in Whitewater
An innocent man (Naboth) died as a result	Vince Foster (and others) mysteriously died
Ahab was deceived by a lying spirit	Bill was accused of lying
Ahab died and Jezebel continued in power	Bill left office and Hillary continued in politics

With respect to America's present and future leaders, America for eight years has fallen into the same despair as Israel did in the days of King Saul. In studying the decisions and leadership methods of President Obama, his prophetic pattern is found in the patterns of King Saul, Israel's first king. While some of these repetitive patterns can be slightly humorous, others are directly related to our time.

Saul was a head taller than other Israelite men, just as President Obama was taller than the average American male. When Saul was "discovered," he was looking for his father's donkeys (the same emblem of Obama's political party). The people had high expectations when Saul came to power, but it was evident right away that he was unprepared for the position. Saul immediately began to reject the spiritual advice and wisdom from men of God, and was warned that his pride would be his downfall. At one point, he sinned and was warned that God was rejecting him. Instead of humbling himself, he became arrogant and requested that the prophet Samuel "make him look good" in the eyes of the people. He was more concerned with popularity than obedience to God.

Perhaps the most noted characteristic of Saul's administration was his out of control debt. Within a few years there was division in the nation, with some loyal to Saul and others loyal to David. Because of Saul's careless leadership, the people were distressed, discontented, and in debt (see 1 Samuel 22:2). In America, before the year 2016, the national debt was out of control, and many were discouraged about the direction the nation was headed, while others were discontented and disillusioned.

THE MARKER OF EACH LEADER

From 1948 to the present, every American president has had at least one specific event that marked his political legacy. For instance, President Truman will be noted as the American president who assisted in forming the state of Israel after the terrible holocaust. President Kennedy refused to be intimidated by the USSR, and he dealt with the Cuban missile crisis. Nixon assisted Israel in the 1973 war, Carter negotiated peace between Israel and Egypt, and Reagan heated up the Cold War so hot that he melted the Iron Curtain over communist Europe. George H. W. Bush successfully liberated Kuwait from further aggression from Saddam Hussein.

Bill Clinton heard that the President of Russia was preparing to crack down on religious groups, such as the Pentecostal groups, which the Russian leader considered a dangerous cult. President Clinton told the Russian leader not to do this, as some of his best friends from Arkansas were Pentecostal. The Russian leader withdrew his plan and later thanked Clinton for his advice.

President G. W. Bush was dealt a hand he never could have antic-ipated—the biggest attack on American soil since Pearl Harbor. This initiated a war in both Afghanistan and Iraq. There was a contro-versy related to Bush's election, as some suggested he "stole it" and was elected illegally. However, what if Gore and Lieberman had won the 2000 election? Following the September 11 terrorist attacks, sev-eral Jewish friends in Israel suggested that if Gore had won, with a Jewish vice president in the White House, the Islamic nations would never have permitted American troops in these Middle East nations. Muslims leaders would have viewed the activity as a Jewish conspiracy to take over the Islamic world.

President Obama certainly kept his promise in 2007 when he said that he would "fundamentally change America." It seems the change included destroying God's idea of tradition marriage, removing all abortion restrictions, signing business-killing regulations, and supporting Israel's enemies.

THE SAUL EFFECT ON AMERICA

It is interesting to note that Saul, Israel's first king, was not from the tribe of Judah, but the tribe of Benjamin (1 Sam. 9:1-2). The kingly scepter was pre-assigned to Judah from the time of Jacob (Gen. 49:10). However, with Israel's hereditary monarchy, if Saul had been from Judah, his oldest son Jonathan would have been crowned king and not David. The Benjamite tribe was the smallest in Israel. It was the Benjamites who, in a rather strange biblical narrative, connected with men from Gibeah, of the tribe of Benjamin, who attempted to gang rape a man hiding in a house, but instead gang raped and killed a female concubine. Benjamin protected the perverted men and was willing to fight with the other tribes to defend this lifestyle (see Judges 20). Eventually, Israel defeated the tribe of Benjamin, reducing their army from twenty-six thousand men to a meager six hundred. To prevent the possible destruction and permanent removal of Benjamin's tribal heritage, the other tribes of Israel gave the young men of Benjamin wives to marry to prevent the tribe from being erased from Israel's history.

For the first time in American history, under President Obama's leadership, gay marriage was promoted and passed into law by the Supreme Court. Acceptance of same sex relations was a legacy of Saul's tribe, Benjamin, as the tribe promoted, permitted, and fought for male prostitution. The legacy of President Obama, to discerning believers, will be that his liberal ideas manifested to change the view of traditional marriage and legalize an abomination, even celebrating the new law by lighting the White House in rainbow colored lights.

THE ARK WAS TAKEN CAPTIVE

The golden Ark of the Covenant indicated the presence of God was dwelling among the people of Israel. In the early days it also held the stone tablets of God's law—the visible sign of His covenant with His people. The Ark was housed in the Tabernacle of Moses in Shiloh and also in the Tabernacle of David on Mount Zion. Later the Ark rested on a stone floor in the Holy of Holies in Solomon's temple, guarded by the Levites and priests. The presence of the Ark was an indicator of God's favor upon the nation. When the Ark rested within its sacred chamber, the people were at peace.

When the divine order of God was disrupted and the Ark was either mishandled or misused, the protective hedge was lifted. This is evident when Uzzah, who was not a priest, touched the Ark with his hands and was instantly struck dead. On another occasion, the sons of the high priest Eli, (who were called sons of Belial for their sins; see 1 Sam. 2:12), removed the Ark from the tabernacle and carried it into battle against the Philistines. The Ark was captured and housed in the idol temple of Dagon (1 Sam. 4 - 5). When this occurred, both sons of Eli were slain and a child born to one of the wives was named Ichabod, meaning "the Glory (of God) has departed" (1 Sam. 4:22).

In 2007, when our newly elected leader said he would fundamentally change America, few people asked for specifics. The media allowed this promise to pass by as a news soundbite. To fundamentally change something means to dig up a foundation and rebuild upon a new foundation. The religious faith of America in the past (Christianity) was no longer important, according to a speech given in 2009 in which the president declared that America is not a Christian nation. It seems that there is now an influential, wealthy inner circle of leaders plotting to revise American history to remove any moral and spiritual beliefs that are contrary to their agenda. With Saul, he had no concern for the loss of the Ark or God's presence, as he was only concerned about maintaining popularity and looking good in the eyes of the people.

THE BATTLES BECAME STUCK

Saul was supposed to be the Commander-in-Chief of the Israeli army. However, as he continued to administer, he became hesitant to go to war. On one occasion, the Philistine giant Goliath taunted Israel, the army, and the king for forty consecutive days, with not one soldier, including the king, stepping up to deal with this vocal enemy. The battle (1 Samuel 17) was stuck and going nowhere.

On the other hand, Saul was more than willing to chase his perceived enemy, David, from village to village and mountain to mountain in an attempt to get him out of the way. Thus, the *real enemies* went unchallenged, but those who *were not* enemies were *made into enemies*, sending the king through caves and over mountains to chase his own shadow.

The prophetic parallel is evident if a person has carefully followed events. Since 2009, the leaders have mistreated long-time allies such as Israel, to promote nuclear deals with Iranian religious leaders who are self-confessed archenemies of both Israel and America. When information was released that the director of the IRS had targeted hundreds of conservative people and political groups before the 2012 election, it was evident that the real enemies of America were being coddled and ignored, while the patriots were treated as enemies.

MAKING WARS WHERE THERE SHOULD BE NO WARS

King Saul's pride and arrogance was so imbedded in his character that the enemies of Israel could engage the king in war and be ignored, while Saul soothed his wounded ego by chasing David and his six hundred men from cave to cave in the Judean wilderness. In today's political circles, politicians get elected, and from the moment they are sworn in, most decisions they make are motivated by how it will impact the next election.

Dangerous issues are ignored by exalting an agenda to appease the base and wealthy financial backers. For example, despite science to the contrary, some people are consumed with climate change, acting as though no generation has ever experienced what we are seeing now. At first the crisis was deemed to be global warming, until the climate cooled down. In order to continue to accommodate an agenda, we then were told that we need to be concerned with climate change. When ISIS terrorists were beheading Christians, the U.S. president refused to say they were a danger. While Iran threatened America and Israel, the U.S. president refused to see them as a grave danger, and signed a deal giving them more than they even wanted. He advised us that the greatest danger in the world is climate change.

We are told the world has never experienced the kind of climate change we are seeing, and that unless we do something now, we will experience droughts, earthquakes, famines, and other such problems. Perhaps the problem is thousands of years of spiritual and biblical ignorance. For example:

- Abraham experienced a severe famine (Gen. 12:10)

- Isaac experienced a severe famine (Gen. 26:1)

- In Jacob's time, a seven-year famine almost wiped out the world (Gen. 41:36)

- Elijah survived a famine that persisted for forty-two months (Luke 4:25)

Imagine Pharaoh standing up in his palace and announcing that global warming is about to wipe everyone out. There have been serious famines, extended droughts, violent earthquakes, and natural disasters since the Fall of Adam. In the New Testament, a severe famine struck Judea and the saints from numerous churches provided financial support for their brethren in need (Acts 11:28-30).

SPIRITS WERE RELEASED TO AFFECT THE LEADERS

Once arrogance and pride became rooted in the heart of Saul, jealousy sprang up and motivated the king to personally attack a righteous lad named David. We read where the Spirit of the Lord departed from Saul and an evil spirit from the Lord (that is, with God's permission) troubled him (1 Sam. 16:14). This Hebrew word *troubled* is *ba'ath* and it means to make afraid or to fear. David's anointing made Saul afraid of David; therefore he retaliated against him and imagined that David was his enemy.

Saul's mental and spiritual weakness began to trickle down to the people dwelling in the nation. People became discouraged. Their debt increased, and in a debt crisis, the borrower is a servant to the lender. When half the population becomes discontent, it leads to a divided commitment.

AMERICANS REACTION TO THE STORMS

Storms can be literal but also metaphorical for problems that can strike suddenly and unexpectedly. To understand how to deal with sudden storms, valuable lessons can be learned from the Bible, where Christ and His disciples encountered a powerful storm on the Sea of Galilee.

In the biblical narrative, Christ instructed His disciples to "go over to the other side" of the lake. In that day this would have required about seven miles of rowing in a boat large enough to accommodate thirteen men and their personal items. As they rowed, the winds became violent and the waves lapped over the boat. The harder they rowed the slower they moved, and Jesus was asleep. The storm that rocked their world rocked Jesus to sleep like an infant in his mother's arms.

What are the possible reactions in this setting? They could turn the boat around and go back where they came from. The problem with going back is that they would still be in the storm. On this lake (I've been there many times), once the wind whips up, it hits the entire lake. Perhaps the ministry team could just grab life jackets and jump ship, especially if the boat is going down. But if you are three miles out in a storm, what other boat is going to pick you up? You might be left in the water for a long time. Then there is the horrible anticipation that, at any moment, the end will come and the team members will be going under. The best solution might be to contact the captain and get some help!

The spiritual, economic, and political storms sweeping America leaves us but one option. Call upon the Captain of the vessel, Jesus

Christ, and ask Him to bring us through the storms, and to give us wise leaders.

MOTIVATING A GENERATION OF SLOTHS

In Proverbs the writer used the word *slothful* eleven times to describe someone we would refer to as lazy. Having been in ministry forty years and working with many different staff members, I have noticed there is a difference between the work ethic of the old and young generations. The older generation arrives on time, works non-stop, and gets the job done day after day. At times, the younger generation would rather talk, chat on social media, or spend time on personal phone calls, thus hindering their focus on the job. How many times have you seen young people text a person next to them who is otherwise being ignored? This is not true in all instances, of course. I'm thankful that we have many dynamic young people in our ministry who are great workers.

Church attendees can fall into two categories: the dedicated and the lukewarm. To the faithful and called, church is not a chore, but a choice; not a burden, but a blessing; not a distraction, but a destination. I have heard many young people say that the reason they do not attend church on Sunday morning is because the service and preaching are not relevant to their lives and needs. They would rather stay up late on Saturday, sleep in late on Sunday, and place the risk of their eternal destiny in their own hands and on their own time.

When God observes unmotivated human beings caught up with themselves and ignoring Him, His Word, and His Presence, how can He motivate us to return to Him? He knows that, without an active covenant, we will be separated from Him eternally.

REWARDS SHOULD MOTIVATE US

If a capable person is always handed something for nothing and never required to work, he will lose motivation. The possibility of being rewarded for your efforts should be a reason to get you off the couch and motivate you to do something. If your employer were to offer a bonus or a pay raise for your extra efforts, would it inspire you to put forth more effort?

It is the idea of a sudden reward that motivates millions of people to spend excessive amounts of money on lottery tickets, hoping they will become America's next overnight millionaire. The selfish motivation of quick money has caused some to become addicted to gambling and others to empty their savings accounts in hopes for a monetary reward.

There is a promise of continual reward for your faith and for serving God and seeking His righteousness. Christ taught that if you seek first God's kingdom and His righteousness, all these things shall be added unto you (Matt. 6:33). Hebrews 11:6 says, "...he that cometh to God must believe that He is, and that He is a rewarder of them that diligently seek him." The Greek word for rewarder is *misthapodotés*, a word used for remuneration for work done, or we would say a reimbursement. When a person works hard to achieve a goal, there is usually a reward for reaching that goal. Football teams, for example, do not practice with the intent of losing. If they believed they would never win, their motivation for tough practices would diminish.

In the Torah, God demonstrated to Israel that certain blessings would follow them if they obeyed His laws and followed His instructions. They would be blessed in the city, in the field, and in their homes. Even plants, trees, and livestock would be healthy. In both Old and New Testaments, there is a blessing imparted to individuals who seek after righteousness. As with natural laws, there are punishments established for breaking the rules that are necessary to prevent someone from stealing, murdering, or committing crimes against others. For a believer, our ultimate reward will be presented at the judgment seat of Christ, where our faithfulness will be honored by Christ himself. Thus rewards should motivate a believer.

WARNINGS SHOULD MOTIVATE

If you were walking in the woods and raised your right foot to take a step, only to see a rattlesnake a yard away from your feet, would you instantly be motivated to turn around and run? If the news reports that an F-4 tornado is headed your way any moment, would you sit and drink coffee or rush to take shelter? If you have common sense, you would do everything possible to protect yourself from danger.

Those in America who have a church and biblical background are observing warning signs of coming selective judgment, yet many are paying little attention to the ominous warnings. Prior to the technology stock bubble in the late 1990s, I heard specialists warning it would crash, but people kept investing. When the mortgage crisis struck, I recall two men saying it was going to crash and cause people to lose their homes. But people kept borrowing. We are warned of an unsustainable national debt, yet we keep printing and borrowing money.

What should a warning do? Warnings are not intended to *scare us,* but to *prepare us.* When Noah knew destruction was coming, by faith and with fear he was moved to prepare an ark for the saving of his house (Heb. 11:7). When Jonah was sent to Nineveh, he arrived after he first had taken a three day ride in a large fish. Normally it was a three day journey but this dripping wet prophet made it in one day. After proclaiming a warning that everyone was going to die if they didn't repent, the entire city repented of every sin imaginable in sackcloth and ashes. God kept His promise and spared the city.

God reveals His mercy in that He warns prior to releasing judgment. God always visits in mercy before He visits in judgment; always extends His hand of grace before lifting His hand in disfavor.

BLESSINGS SHOULD MOTIVATE

Consider what motivates a person to repentance. I believe there are three reasons people repent:

- Because the person is reproved (KJV) or convicted by the Holy Spirit (John 16:8)

- Because of the fear of spending eternity in hell (Jude 23)

- Because of the goodness of the Lord (Rom. 2:4)

But blessings do not always motivate people toward obedience. Compare this to the work ethic. When people expect everything to continue as usual and everything is given to them, many lose their gratefulness and their motivation to work. They become irresponsible. If somebody else bought the car they drive, it doesn't matter if they wreck it. If they have no investment in the home they're living in, it doesn't matter if it falls apart.

In the same manner, if we experience the blessings of God without repentance, then there is no need to repent. We believe everything will continue as it has, even if we are disobedient. Sometimes God, in His mercy toward us, will bring judgment to turn the hearts of disobedient people back to Him. This is the primary reason for any judgment cycle upon a person or a nation—to lead them to repentance.

CHAPTER 6

PATTERNS OF THE FALL FESTIVALS

THE SEVEN APPOINTED festivals of the Lord conceal both practical and prophetic elements—from the practical aspect of rain and harvest cycles, to the revelation of specific, major events related to the Messiah, His redemptive plan, and His future kingdom on Earth. The order of the festivals also conceals often-missed prophetic patterns that reveal the *order of future events* related to biblical prophecy.

These festivals are called *the feasts of the Lord* (Lev. 23:2), *the time appointed* (Exod. 23:15), *holy convocations* (Lev. 23:4), *solemn feasts* (2 Chron. 2:4) and *set feasts* (Ezra 3:5). God revealed the names, order, and purpose of these festivals to Moses in the wilderness following Israel's exodus from Egypt. Each festival commemorates a major event in the life of the Hebrews, from their departure from Egypt until they entered the Promised Land. The seven feasts, listed in order are:

The English/ Hebrew Name	The Jewish Month	The English Equivalent
Passover / Pesach	1st month—14th day	March / April
Unleavened/ Hag HaMatzah	1st month— 15th–21st days	March / April
First Fruits / Bikkurim	1st month—day after Sabbath of Unleavened Bread	March / April

Pentecost / Shavuot	50 days from first fruits	May / June
Trumpets / Yom Teruah	7th month—1st day	September / October
Atonement / Yom Kippur	7th month—10th day	September / October
Tabernacles / Sukkot	7th month— 15th – 21st days	September / October

The first feast of the Lord was Passover, which commemorated Israel's departure from Egypt. This feast reminded the people how God protected Israel's firstborn from the death angel at midnight, passing over the homes marked by the lamb's blood (see Exodus 12). The next morning, as Israel prepared for their departure from Egyptian slavery and gathered for the journey back to their Promised Land, the Hebrew families had no time to properly prepare leaven in their dough for bread. Thus the bread they prepared was unleavened bread, hence the feast with the corresponding name. The very next day began a special time set aside to mark the barley harvest—the season of their redemption—called the Festival of First Fruits.

From the day following the Passover Sabbath, Moses was instructed to initiate a count for seven days and continue this count for seven consecutive weeks. This set time is known as the *Feast of Weeks*. Later it would be identified in Christ's time as *Pentecost*, a Greek word for *fifty*, as the timing of the 49 days (7 days times 7 weeks) came to a climax (was fully come, see Acts 2:1-4 KJV) on the fiftieth day after Passover. The Feast of Weeks was marked to commemorate the time Moses ascended Mount Sinai to receive the Law of the Lord.

The first three Spring festivals occur on the first month of the Jewish religious calendar. Pentecost is celebrated on the third month. Four months later, on the seventh month, three appointed seasons were designated by the Lord for Israel: the Feast of Trumpets, the Day of Atonement, and the Feast of Tabernacles. The festival of blowing of trumpets was a holy convocation that initiated a nine-day period of preparation for the Day of Atonement, when the High Priest would make intercession for himself, the Levites, and the Israelites. This was a day of fasting and humility, accompanied by the fear of the

Lord upon the nation. Once atonement was made and Israel passed the repentance test, five days later, on the fifteenth day of the month, began the festival of Tabernacles. This continued for seven consecutive days.

There is not much information in the Torah to explain why the Lord initiated Feast of Trumpets, other than it would be a picture of *a major prophetic event to occur in the future.* The Day of Atonement was established by the Lord as a yearly examination of Israel, to remind them that He is the judge and has power to forgive or condemn, and bless or judge them, based upon their repentance and obedience to His laws. Feast of Tabernacles was a reminder to the Jews of the forty years that Israel spent dwelling in tents in the wilderness. During the week of Tabernacles, devout Jews build a sukkot (a booth) outside of their apartments in Jerusalem or their homes in the other regions of Israel, and follow specific customs and rules laid down by God and by Jewish rabbinical interpretation regarding this season of God.

FULFILLMENT AND NON-FULFILLMENT OF THE FESTIVALS

When one studies the prophetic significance of these seven appointed times, it becomes evident that each was given to paint a clear picture of the entire redemptive plan and kingdom of the Jewish Messiah. For example, Passover was the first yearly celebration that Israel was to honor. On the first Passover, a young lamb without blemish was slain and its blood placed on three places: the upper, left, and right posts of the outer door of the house. The lamb was then roasted and the people were instructed to *eat all of it.* The blood of the lamb prevented the angel of death from entering any home of a Hebrew, thus preserving the lives of the firstborn sons (see Exodus 12). The Passover lamb was fulfilled in Christ, who was called the "Lamb of God that takes away the sins of the world" (John 1:29). Three crosses were part of the crucifixion narrative, reminding us that three marks of blood were on each Hebrew door post in Egypt. The blood of Christ was required to seal the redemption of those who would believe upon Him, and the stripes He carried through His scourging became the stripes of healing for those who would believe (Isa. 53:5; 1 Pet. 2:24). Just as the lamb's body and blood in Egypt provided a twofold atonement of protection from death and physical sickness, Christ's atoning work included His blood freeing us from sin and death, and His body being bruised for our spiritual, physical, and emotional healing (Isa. 53:1-12).

Christ lived in a human body that was capable of being tempted and sinning. Although He was tempted (Matt. 4:1-11), Christ willingly resisted all forms of sin and refused to participate in any act of disobedience; thus He was without sin (see 2 Cor. 5:21). In the New Testament, leaven is considered a picture of a sinful lifestyle that continues to grow when a person does not repent. Bread without leaven represents a life free from sin; thus the yearly commemoration of Unleavened Bread is a picture of Christ dying as a sinless sacrifice.

The next appointed season immediately following Unleavened Bread is the Festival of First Fruits which marks the beginning of the barley harvest. On the first day of this festival the high priest in Jerusalem would arise in the morning, step into a barley field somewhere in the Kidron Valley, and mark the first ripened barley. He would take a sickle and cut a handful of grain, stems and all. At the temple, he would offer a lamb and the first ripened barley harvest. Christ fulfilled this imagery as He arose from the dead on the morning of First Fruits. At His resurrection, numerous saints of God who had died in Jerusalem were also raised from the grave with Him. Matthew speaks of this event in Matthew 27:52-53:

> "And the graves were opened; and many bodies of the saints which slept arose, and came out of the graves after His resurrection, and went into the holy city and appeared unto many."

These raised saints were the first fruits of Christ's own resurrection! The high priest harvests only a small section and not the entire field of barley. Matthew said "many bodies" that slept; he did not say *all*, as this would have been multiplied thousands. First Fruits is not about a complete harvest; it is about setting aside a portion of the harvest in order to sanctify the remaining part of the field. Christ raised a first fruits group of righteous from the dead to give assurance to all who would die in Him, that He would one day raise them all from the dead!

Clearly, Christ specifically fulfilled the first three festivals, in the actual order in which they fall: Passover represents the crucifixion, Unleavened Bread represents that He is sinless, and First Fruits represents resurrection from the grave.

Given the divine order, the next Feast of the Lord that must conceal a prophetic event is the Feast of Weeks, or Pentecost. Before ascending to heaven, Christ instructed His followers to tarry in the city of Jerusalem until they were endued (literally clothed) with power from on high (Luke 24:49). This they did, as is evident when Luke recorded the events that occurred on the very day of the Pentecost festival. The Holy Spirit descended and appeared as cloven tongues like fire and baptized the entire group, providing them with a prayer language that allowed them to supernaturally communicate with God (Acts 2:4). The original "Pentecost" was when Moses went to the top of Mount Sinai and met God in the fire and the cloud, accompanied by thunder and lightning (see Exodus 19). During the Pentecost of Acts, the fire of God came, the voice of God was heard through the tongues of the people, and the church was born!

On the day of Pentecost, there were conversions to Christ, water baptisms, and fulfillment of the promise of the infilling of the Holy Spirit (Acts 2). This represents the three primary messages that we are to preach: go into all of the world and preach the Gospel, baptize believers in water, and encourage believers to receive the baptism of the Holy Spirit (Mark 16:15-18). Pentecost authenticated the resurrection of Christ through the power of the Holy Spirit. Today the true, anointed church has an assignment to spread the Gospel to all nations, and then the end will come (Matt. 24:14).

THREE FESTIVALS YET UNFULFILLED

Notice that God has prophetically followed a perfect order for the first four festivals. It stands to reason that He will fulfill the three fall festivals *in the very order* in which they were revealed to Moses. These would be Trumpets, Atonement, and Tabernacles.

Those familiar with Hebraic teachings often ask what festival or festival pattern are we in prophetically at this time. Since the initiation of the church at Pentecost and the forming of the Body of Christ on Earth through the *ekklesia*, or the called out ones, we have been living continually at Pentecost (or the church age). The next festival in the divine order is Trumpets. There is no indication, during the nearly 2,000 years of church history, that the pattern of Trumpets has ever been fulfilled in any form.

Christ asked His disciples why they said, "yet four months and then comes the harvest" (John 4:35). Any Jewish man would have understood that Christ was referring to the four literal months between Pentecost and Trumpets. Pentecost falls on the third month (Sivan) and Trumpets begins on the seventh month (Tishrei); they are four months apart. The harvest crops in Israel that indicate the fall months are ahead are the olives, grapes, figs, and pomegranates. Christ was metaphorically speaking of the harvest of souls for His kingdom. He stated that the fields (the world) were ready for the Gospel, and His disciples must set out to reap the grain (souls) into the kingdom. Jesus often used *natural* surroundings to teach *spiritual* lessons.

THE ORDER OF FUTURE EVENTS

When viewing prophecy from a literal perspective and decoding the symbolism of the apocalyptic prophets (Daniel, Zechariah, and John), there are at least three events that remain to be fulfilled during the Gentile dominion of the world's governments:

1. The return of Christ for the church, called the "catching away" and "gathering together"

2. The rise of a ten king confederacy controlled by the Antichrist during the Tribulation

3. The return of Christ to Earth to defeat Satan and evil, and set up a thousand-year Kingdom

When God's appointed time to complete the Pentecost cycle has reach its fullness, the church age will end with the return of Christ for the church. When the Gospel is preached to the nations, the outpouring of the Spirit sweeps the world, and when the grace of God has been dispensed, the return of Christ to catch away the believers will occur. As Christ said:

> "This gospel of the kingdom shall be preached in all the world as a witness unto all nations; and then shall the end come."
>
> – MATTHEW 24:14 (KJV)

The global preaching of the Gospel brings in the fullness of the Gospel which, in one day, will climax with the return of Christ for redeemed believers around the globe. Some disagree that the seven-year Tribulation will begin at the culmination of the church age. Some teach that the church must go through part or all of the Tribulation, and then Christ will return. I will show you, based upon the *divine order* of the festivals, that God will initiate prophetic events in conjunction with the three fall festivals.

One of the central features of Christ's return will be the blowing of trumpets. Paul taught that when the Lord descends to Earth, He does so with "a shout, the voice of the archangel and the trump of God..." (1 Thess. 4:16). Paul again alluded to a trumpet blast when he wrote, "...we shall be changed at the sound of the last trump, for the trumpet shall sound and the dead shall be raised incorruptible..." (1 Cor. 15:52). The next festival that has not been fulfilled, but must have a prophetic fulfillment is Trumpets. Moses wrote:

> "Speak unto the children of Israel, saying, in the seventh month, in the first day of the month, shall ye have a Sabbath, a memorial of blowing of trumpets, an holy convocation. Ye shall do no servile work therein: but ye shall offer an offering made by fire unto the LORD."
>
> – LEVITICUS 23:24-25 (KJV)

The Feast of Trumpets is a clear picture of the trumpet of God that sounds and brings God's family into a season of rest, called in Leviticus a *Sabbath*. Paul in Hebrews speaks of this time as a "rest for God's people" (Heb. 4:9). Paul uses the word "rest" eleven times in Hebrews (3:11, 18; 4:1, 3 (twice), 4, 5, 8, 9, 10, 11). Ten times the Greek word "rest" is *katapausis*, a word meaning to repose and lie down for a rest. In verse 4:9, the rest that remains for God's people is the Greek word *sabbatismos*, which refers to the believers entering into their rest when they arrive in heaven on Trumpets. The blowing of trumpets introduced a Sabbath rest and a holy convocation that freed all people from their labors! This is the imagery of Christ returning in the clouds with the sound of the trumpets, to raise the dead and catch up the living to meet Him in the air.

YOU CAN'T CHANGE GOD'S ORDER

I have dear friends who teach that the next order of events will be the revealing of the Antichrist, the Great Tribulation, and then the return of Christ to catch away believers, which is a post-Tribulation belief. However, God's divine order cannot be reversed. There can be no doubt that the Day of Atonement is a clear picture of God's judgments in the Tribulation. Jewish commentary on Atonement indicates there will be three types of people on that day: the totally righteous, the totally unrighteous, and those caught in the middle who are neither righteous nor unrighteous. During Atonement, God weighs the sins of each individual and the nation to determine if they deserve forgiveness or judgment. The sentencing is based upon repentance or the lack thereof of those being weighed.

When reading the book of Revelation, we can see that all three types of individuals will be on Earth during the seven-year Tribulation. There is the righteous remnant in Israel, namely the 144,000 Jews that are sealed with the seal of God and protected from God's wrath (see Rev. 7). A second group—the vast majority—will blaspheme God and refuse to repent (Rev. 9:20; 16:11; 16:21). There will be a third group of people who were not prepared for the return of Christ and were left on Earth to endure the early part of the Tribulation. They are a multitude that make their robes white in the blood of the Lamb and come out of the Great Tribulation (Rev. 7:14). The righteous (remnant), the unrighteous, and the lukewarm must choose to either die a martyr or accept the mark of the beast. The Tribulation is clearly concealed in the patterns of the Day of Atonement.

If a prophetic minister teaches that the Tribulation must precede the rapture of the church, he has changed the order by placing the Day of Atonement before the Feast of Trumpets. This would be like replacing Passover with First Fruits, and having Passover become the third festival instead of its God-given position as the first. The plan of God would be disrupted and God's patterns would be out of order. You must have Passover (the crucifixion), then Unleavened Bread (Christ in the tomb), then First Fruits (the resurrection that follows Christ's death). Pentecost could not have occurred until Christ rose from the dead and became seated as the High Priest in heaven. Jesus told His disciples that if He did not go away (back to the Father), the Comforter (the Holy Spirit) could not come; but if He went away, He would send the Holy Spirit to them (see John 16:7). Pentecost cannot precede Passover, as redemption comes first and then Spirit baptism. In Egypt, Israel was saved by the blood; the following day they went into the sea or the water of baptism, and weeks later they received the Law at Pentecost. This order is redemption, death and resurrection (baptism in water), and the Holy Spirit baptism (Pentecost).

Since the Holy Spirit was given to the disciples on the exact day of the feast of Pentecost (Acts 2:1), then the order of God, for the first four feasts, remained in perfect prophetic order without any alteration. To place the Tribulation (Day of Atonement) before Trumpets (the rapture) is to change God's flowchart of prophetic events to fulfill a particular theological belief. The fall prophetic pattern must be:

1. Trumpets—the return of the Lord *for* the saints with the sound of the trump of God

2. Atonement—the rise of the Antichrist and the seven-year Tribulation

3. Tabernacles—the setting up of the Kingdom of God on Earth when Christ returns *with* the saints

If Atonement is the wrath of God and His judgment being poured out on the ungodly, then the next prophetic event following Atonement is Tabernacles. This is a picture of the Kingdom of Christ ruling on Earth for a thousand years (Rev. 20:4). Christ ruling from Jerusalem as King of kings cannot precede the Feast of Trumpets; neither can it be repositioned before the Day of Atonement. Feast of Trumpets is first, Atonement is second, and Tabernacles is third—in that order!

WHAT DOES THIS DIVINE ORDER MEAN?

Since the seven Jewish Festivals hold a practical purpose (rain and harvest cycles), a spiritual picture (of events related to ancient Israel), and a prophetic imagery of events to come, how does this divine order alter various theological theories related to the return of Christ?

First, there is a difference between the two natures of Christ the Messiah; He is both the *suffering servant* and the *ruling King*. As the suffering servant, His symbol is a *lamb* that was slain (Rev. 5:6). However, when Christ prepares to receive the church, judge the world, and return to set up His rule from Jerusalem, He will transition to the nature of a *lion*—the Lion of the Tribe of Judah (Rev. 5:5). The Apostle John heard Christ identified as the "Lion of Judah." The angel also stated that Christ was the "Root of David," and Christ had prevailed (was worthy, see verse 9) to open the seals. The mentioning of David is significant, since King David (Israel's second king, but first king from the tribe of Judah) was promised a kingly ruling dynasty (2 Sam. 7:13-16). Thus, the three Spring festivals link Christ with the suffering Lamb and the three fall festivals identify him as the Lion of the Tribe of Judah.

Second, the fall festivals clear up the order of events: the rapture, the Tribulation, and millennial reign of Christ—in that order. Since these festivals align with the future kingdom and the Messianic king, then Trumpets reveals the King returning for His bride (the church); Atonement reveals the King's judgment against the Gentile nations;

and Tabernacles reveals Christ ruling as King on Earth for a thousand years.

In the Psalms, David and other inspired writers identify the Lord as the true King. We read, "I have set my king upon the holy hill of Zion" (Psa. 2:6). The Psalmist added, "The Lord is King forever and ever; the heathen are perished of his land" (Psa. 10:16). The entire 22nd Psalm was written, according to some scholars, when David brought the Ark of the Covenant back to Jerusalem. He cried out, "Lift up your heads, O ye gates; and be lifted up you everlasting doors; and the King of glory shall come in" (Psa. 24:7-10).

Christ is a High Priest after the order of Melchizedek (Psa. 110:4; Heb. 5:6; 7:17, 21). In Scripture there are three priestly lineages. The first is Melchizedek, the second is Aaron, and the third is Zadok. Melchizedek was the only true priest of God living on Earth in the days of Abraham (see Gen. 14). In Moses' time, when God established the Levitical priesthood, Aaron from the tribe of Levi was appointed high priest in the early stages of Israel's journey in the wilderness. From that moment until the time of David, the descendants of Aaron who served as priests were called the sons of Aaron, and his priesthood the Aaronic priesthood (see Exodus 28).

The third priestly linage was Zadok, first mentioned in 2 Samuel 8:17. Zadok and the Levites cared for the Ark when David was being exiled from leadership by his own son Absalom (2 Sam. 15). Zadok was a faithful priest to David in a time when many were rejecting him for his sin, and his own sons were in rebellion as they attempted to seize the throne. Zadok and Nathan the prophet anointed Solomon to replace David as king (1 Kings 1:45).

According to Ezekiel, in the future Kingdom of the Messiah, a massive holy temple will be built in Jerusalem and be overseen by the sons of Zadok. This is God honoring the sons of Zadok who cared for the sanctuary of God in a time when Israel went astray; therefore, they shall be assigned in the millennial reign to supervise the priesthood in the temple (see Ezekiel 44:15; 48:11).

THE MELCHIZEDEK CONNECTION

Why did God pattern the priestly ministry of Christ after the order of Melchizedek? Remember, God has a set order and once He establishes the precise pattern, that flow is systematic and unbreakable. He alone has set the boundaries of each pattern. Melchizedek's identity is somewhat mysterious. Jewish rabbis tend to teach that he was Shem, the righteous son of Noah, who still would have been living in the time of Abraham. The name Melchizedek comes from two Hebrew words: *melek*, which is a chief magistrate, or a word later used for a king over 2,500 times in the Bible. The second word is *sadeq*, meaning *to be just or righteous*. The root denotes being conformed to a certain ethical and moral standard. Thus the name can mean, "king of righteousness." In Melchizedek's time, the city he was overseeing as a king and priest was called Salem, later called Jerusalem (Gen. 14:18). The English word Salem in Hebrew is Shalem, meaning peaceful. One can see this name Salem in the English spelling of Jerusalem.

Hebrews 7:1 indicates that Melchizedek was "king of Salem and priest of the Most High God." When God established the priesthood for Israel and later permitted a monarchy, the position of priest and king were separated into two distinct offices, always led by two different men. Both positions were inherited—that is, passed from father to son. However, outside of Melchizedek, no priest could be a king and no king could be a priest. Perhaps the priestly duties, responsibilities, and rituals at the tabernacle and temple were too numerous, and the focus of a priest must be to minister to the Lord continually. Priests dealt with God, but kings dealt with the people. A minister cannot spend more time with people than in intimacy with God and expect dynamic spiritual results.

Christ's priestly order was the pattern of Melchizedek. Thus, Christ is a Lamb and a Lion, or a priest (with the humility and submission of a lamb) and a king (with the dominion and authority of the lion). Three festivals are linked to a lamb: Passover (redemptive blood), Unleavened Bread (no leaven in the bread), and First Fruits (the first harvest from the field). Three fall festivals are linked to the blast of trumpets, the judgment where people choose life or death, and the Jews and Gentiles uniting in a future Kingdom in Israel.

TABERNACLES AND THE KINGDOM

From apocalyptic passages, the Tribulation lasts seven years, and at the conclusion of the Tribulation, Christ the Messiah and King returns to Earth (see Revelation 19). This imagery is verified in the Torah, where Moses is repeating instructions to the children of Israel regarding the feasts of the Lord. An interesting clue is concealed within this statement:

> "And Moses commanded them, saying: "At the end of every seven years, at the appointed time in the year of release, at the Feast of Tabernacles, when all Israel comes to appear before the LORD your God in the place which He chooses, you shall read this law before all Israel in their hearing. Gather the people together, men and women and little ones, and the stranger who is within your gates, that they may hear and that they may learn to fear the LORD your God and carefully observe all the words of this law, and that their children, who have not known it, may hear and learn to fear the LORD your God as long as you live in the land which you cross the Jordan to possess."
>
> – DEUTERONOMY 31:10-13 (NKJV)

Notice at the end of every seven years there is a release! At the conclusion of the seven-year Tribulation, the Earth and its inhabitants will be released from Satan, the Antichrist, the false prophet, and from wicked men marked as tares who are removed from Earth by Christ when He returns. The Hebrew word "release" in Deuteronomy is *shemitah,* and refers to the end of every seven years, when a remission of labor is announced and permitted. The word "shemitah" is also used in Deut. 15:2 and 9, and translates as *release* in the KJV.

Using the fall festival pattern, it appears that Christ will return for the overcoming church to raise the dead in Christ and *release the living saints* from this mortal body of flesh during the beginning of a specific fall festival season (the year is unknown). Then seven years later, Christ will return to *release the world* from Satan's power in the fall months, with Tabernacles being the celebration when the elect will rejoice to see the Messiah.

In the Torah, at the time of release, all Israel appears before the Lord. The law of the three main festivals was that all males over twenty must appear at the Feast of Unleavened Bread (Passover), Feast of Weeks (Pentecost), and Tabernacles. Notice that only males attend (Exod. 23:17; Deut. 16:16).

Passover is our redemption, where the Lamb of God, Christ Jesus, redeemed us to God through the new covenant. Pentecost is our individual Holy Spirit baptism, as Acts 2:1-4 indicates that the Spirit was poured out and the church was birthed on the very day of the festival in Jerusalem (around seven days after Christ ascended to heaven). The Feast of Tabernacles is the raising of the dead (Tribulation martyrs) and the Kingdom of Messiah promised to those who would faithfully follow Him (Rev. 20:1-4).

At the end of every seven years, on Tabernacles, everybody—men, women, and children—all came to Jerusalem to the temple for a major celebration. The Lord used the phrase "gather the people together." This will be the gathering of the wheat after the tares (children of Satan) have been separated from the harvest field (the Earth):

> "Therefore as the tares are gathered and burned in the fire, so it will be at the end of the age. The Son of Man will send out His angels, and they will gather out of His kingdom all things that offend, and those who practice lawlessness, and will cast them into the furnace of fire..."
>
> – MATTHEW 13:40-42 (NKJV)

During the thousand years, all nations will make a yearly pilgrimage to Jerusalem during the Feast of Tabernacles to celebrate the Lord the King (Zech. 14:16).

The most significant Tabernacle's imagery is found in the narrative of Christ's transfiguration. We read:

> "And after six days Jesus taketh Peter, James, and John his brother, and bringeth them up into an high mountain apart, and was transfigured before them: and his face did shine as the

sun, and his raiment was white as the light. And, behold, there appeared unto them Moses and Elias talking with him. Then answered Peter, and said unto Jesus, Lord, it is good for us to be here: if thou wilt, let us make here three tabernacles; one for thee, and one for Moses, and one for Elias."

– Matthew 17:1-4 (KJV)

Peter, James, and John were with Christ on this occasion. Why would Peter suddenly suggest building three tabernacles—one for Jesus, one for Moses, and one for Elijah? The Greek word for "tabernacles" is *skene*, which refers to a tent. The festival of Tabernacles was celebrated yearly, reminding the Hebrews they once lived in the wilderness, in *tents*, for forty years.

The transfiguration occurred "after six days," meaning on the seventh day. Tabernacles is celebrated for seven days, and it is likely that Christ's transfiguration occurred on the last day of the Feast of Tabernacles. This is important when we understand Christ's teaching on the resurrection, which He taught before this event. In John chapter 6, Christ mentioned the raising of the dead four times (6:39, 40, 44, 54). In all four references, he says they will be raised "at the last day." Not the last days, a term used for the time of the end, but the last *day*. Just what is the last day?

If the transfiguration occurred on the last day of Tabernacles, and suddenly Peter awoke seeing Elijah and Moses, perhaps his mind began to swirl as he tried to comprehend the moment. Christ is glowing white, Elijah, a prophet transported alive to heaven who was expected to return and announce the Messiah's Kingdom is there, and Moses is standing with them. I believe Peter thought the resurrection of the righteous had occurred and he was prepared to build the booths, or tabernacles, as this would have been the conclusion of the festival where Jewish families spend seven days living outside of their homes in man-made booths. Peter might have assumed that the Kingdom had now come and Christ was preparing for His rule on Earth. After all, prophets such as Daniel and Zechariah had previewed the King-Messiah ruling the Earth from Jerusalem (Dan. 2:44-45; Zech. 14:9, 16-17).

Feast of Trumpets reveals Christ as the bridegroom receiving His bride. Atonement is Christ the heavenly priest initiating judgment on the earth for shedding the blood of the righteous (Rev. 18:24). Feast of Tabernacles is the season where Christ the Heavenly Priest repositions from Priest to the King of kings! That is the order.

CHAPTER 7

YOM HAKESEH: THE MYSTERY OF THE HIDDEN DAY

NYONE WHO CAN read is able to pick up a Bible, in one of many translations, and read the words printed on the paper. The stories are simple, practical, and easy to understand. The parables, called the "mysteries of the Kingdom," are explained by Christ in numerous instances. The New Testament doctrine of the Apostles and Christ is simple for most people to understand. However, the scriptures contain "prophetic layers" that conceal biblical mysteries in the types, shadows, patterns, and cycles that must be comprehended by spiritual understanding. Isaiah wrote:

> "Even from the beginning I have declared it to you; before it came to pass I proclaimed it to you, lest you should say, 'My idol has done them, and my carved image and my molded image have commanded them. You have heard; see all this, and will you not declare it? I have made you hear new things from this time, even hidden things, and you did not know them."
>
> – ISAIAH 48:5-6 (NKJV)

THINGS HIDDEN FROM US

Some things are hidden from us during our lifetime. With few exceptions, people do not know the *exact day* and *hour* of their own death.

Elijah understood the day he would be taken to heaven (see 2 Kings 2). Christ understood the patterns of both His death near Passover and His resurrection after three days and nights in the grave (Matt. 12:40). Personally, I prefer not to know the year and day that I will die, as there could be much dread and anguish over separating from family as the time approached.

Trouble that will be in our path and the ways in which it will impact us is seldom revealed. The exception would be if we are given an advanced warning of danger, such as when Paul boarded the ship for Rome (see Acts 27), or when he was warned of his future arrest during an upcoming trip to celebrate a festival in Jerusalem (see Acts 21:11). Job is an example of how trouble can strike suddenly and unexpectedly, and in the process cause great grief and pain (see Job 1 and 2).

A third and most important hidden event is the day and hour when Christ will return. Just as the men and women in the days of Noah and Lot were caught off guard and unaware of the flood and the fire, no man or woman living on Earth will know the day or the hour of Christ's return (see Matt. 24:36; Mark 13:32).

A common question is: why has God concealed the day and hour of Christ's return? I believe there are three answers to that question. First, God uses this to impart *anticipation*, the seed of which is planted in the hearts of believers worldwide when they hear the words, *Jesus is coming soon*. Second, if you believe Christ could return at any time, the expectancy leads to a selfless and more righteous lifestyle. This causes a believer to continue in their faith, search themselves, and guard their hearts from unrighteousness. John wrote about the appearing of the Lord and how, at Christ's return, we would be like Him (1 John 3:1-2). He then added:

> "And everyone who has this hope in Him purifies himself, just as he is pure."
>
> – 1 JOHN 3:3 (NKJV)

A third reason for not revealing the exact time of Christ's return is that this concealed event helps us encourage others to follow the Lord and be obedient to His Word, as we remind them of the last days, the events that will come upon the earth, and the blessings of entering the kingdom. Christ instructed us to watch and pray, since we know not the hour of His return (Matt. 25:13).

THE PATTERN OF YOM HAKESEH

One of the lesser-taught occurrences known in Rabbinical circles that provides imagery of the concealment of Christ's return is called Yom HaKeseh. To understand this phrase, a review of God's cosmic calendar is necessary. In the creation narrative, Moses wrote:

> "And God said, Let there be lights in the firmament of the heaven to divide the day from the night; and let them be for signs, and for seasons, and for days, and years."
>
> – GENESIS 1:14 (NKJV)

> "He appointed the moon for seasons: the sun knows its going down."
>
> – PSALMS 104:19 (NKJV)

The three cosmic lights are the sun, the moon, and the stars. The sun was the greater light created to rule by day, and the moon the lesser light to rule by night. The earth rotates in the heavens for 365.25 days to complete one solar year. The moon circles the earth, moving from darkness to a full moon and from full back to darkness in 29.5 days, marking a lunar month. The stars were positioned to give direction to men in early travel. The yearly and monthly cycles and the appearing and reappearing of the moon assisted in determining the months in the year and the seasons assigned to the festivals.

In Genesis 1:14, Moses taught that the cosmic lights were for signs and seasons. The word "seasons" is *moed*, a Hebrew word used when speaking of a Jewish festival (*moadim* being plural and referring to festivals). The word "signs" is *oth* and refers to a miracle or a token, indicating that the cosmic lights would serve as signs to those living on Earth. Generations later, Christ forecast there would be "signs in the sun, the moon, and the stars" (Luke 21:25) indicating strange cosmic activity marking the season of His return. Of the seven major Jewish festivals, perhaps the most mysterious is the fifth festival of the Lord called the Memorial of Trumpets.

I call the holy convocation of the Memorial of Blowing of Trumpets the "mystery festival," and here is why. The Lord instructed Moses concerning the name and rituals, but there is nothing to indicate the purpose of this festival. We read:

> "Then the Lord spoke to Moses, saying, "Speak to the children of Israel, saying: 'In the seventh month, on the first day of the month, you shall have a Sabbath-rest, a memorial of blowing of trumpets, a holy convocation. You shall do no customary work on it; and you shall offer an offering made by fire to the Lord."
>
> – LEVITICUS 23:23-25 (NKJV)

In the Scripture there are three Hebrew words translated as trumpet: *teruah*, *shofar*, and *chatsotserah*. The shofar is traditionally the small, curved horn of a ram, while the larger shofars are the horns of an antelope. The chatsotserah is a trumpet made of silver, brass, or gold (see Num. 10:2). These were the trumpets blown in Joshua 6:4, when the priests blew seven trumpets at the conquest of Jericho. The word for the trumpets blown on the festival of Trumpets is *teruah*, which refers to a battle cry, a joyful sound, or an alarm. It is a loud blast that awakens a person.

NOW LIVING AT PENTECOST

In Revelation chapters two and three, Christ addressed seven of the largest and most influential churches that existed at the time of the Apostle John. In Revelation chapter one, Christ stood before the seven candlesticks in a priestly-style white garment. In chapters two and three are individual messages to seven churches. In chapter four is a transition, as John hears a voice of a trumpet saying, "Come up here" (Rev. 4:1). In Revelation 4:1-2, there is an imagery of a trumpet-type voice issuing a command to come up, with John immediately being in heaven in the Spirit.

In Revelation chapter one, the resurrected Christ is the imagery of the first fruits of the dead, the one who "was dead but is alive forevermore" (Rev. 1:18). He rose from the grave when the very Festival of First Fruits was beginning in Jerusalem. In chapters two and three, the imagery is Pentecost, as Pentecost is certainly the church age.

After the final message to the seventh church, John wrote, "After these things I heard a voice." This refers to the time after the church age, which will cease at the moment of the rapture. The Spirit said that John would now see things that would be hereafter, which also moved the scene from Pentecost to Trumpets. There is First Fruits (Christ being seen alive—Rev. 1), then Pentecost (the church age—Rev. 2 and 3), then Trumpets (the rapture—Rev. 4:1-2). Pentecost begins in early Summer and Trumpets at the beginning of the fall months, which also introduces the rain cycles for winter. This imagery is found in the epistle of James:

> "Therefore be patient, brethren, until the coming of the Lord. See how the farmer waits for the precious fruit of the earth, waiting patiently for it until it receives the early and latter rain. You also be patient. Establish your hearts, for the coming of the Lord is at hand."
>
> – JAMES 5:7-8 (NKJV)

The fruit is not natural food; rather, this alludes to the souls of mankind that will be converted and caught up to heaven (the harvest) at the return of the Lord. The rain is a metaphor for the outpouring of the Holy Spirit (Acts 2:16-17) which climaxes during the church age, which is Pentecost. The coming of the Lord must follow to fulfill the next festival order, Trumpets, which represents the rapture.

To further demonstrate that the Apocalypse flows according to the seven festival patterns, consider what occurs after the trumpet scene in Revelation 4:1-2. The next order would be judgment on the Day of Atonement, which can be viewed in Revelation chapter 6, when the seven-sealed scroll is opened as the Lamb (Christ) breaks one seal at a time. The Tribulation judgments last seven years; and on the seventh year, the saints experience a shemitah in heaven at the marriage supper of the Lamb. This is the last year of the seven-year Tribulation. Just as each seventh day brought a rest from work, so we will rest from all of our labors.

During the Festival of Unleavened Bread, no leaven is permitted in the home or in any baked bread for seven days. However, at Pentecost, the priest would take newly gathered grains of wheat, crush them, and sift the flour ten times before the flour is baked into two loaves of bread. In the parable of the wheat and tares, the wheat are the children of the Kingdom (Matt. 13:38). The two loaves at Pentecost represent the Jews and Gentiles, as when the church was born on Earth, both Jews and Gentiles who believed in Christ became one family or "one new man" (Eph. 2:15).

Since leaven is a metaphor for sin, why would the Pentecost festival, weeks later, use leaven in the bread? This was the festival marking the birth of the church, and God requires believers to live free from a life of sin. This is further complicated when reading the parable in Matthew 13:33, where the kingdom is like three measures of leaven that cause dough to rise. It seems that leaven is sometimes used as a negative metaphor, and at other times a positive. The reason for the bread and leaven parable is that the growth of the kingdom (and the church) would be so swift that it could be compared to leaven in bread. Once the gospel of the Kingdom has been preached throughout the world as a witness to all nations, then the end will come (Matt. 24:14). When the church age ends, with the blast of the trumpet of God, the Tribulation will soon follow.

THE DAY OF REMEMBRANCE

Below are the verses that allude to the blowing of trumpets, or the Festival of Trumpets:

> "Then the Lord spoke to Moses, saying, "Speak to the children of Israel, saying: 'In the seventh month, on the first day of the month, you shall have a Sabbath-rest, a memorial of blowing of trumpets, a holy convocation. You shall do no customary work on it; and you shall offer an offering made by fire to the Lord."
> – LEVITICUS 23:23-15 (NKJV)

The text indicated several important instructions on this day. This memorial is set on the first day of the seventh month. In Scripture the number seven marks *completion* or *perfection*. On this festival, one hundred trumpet blasts are blown on this single day. The entire day from sunrise to sunset is a Sabbath-rest, meaning that no work would be done on that day.

When Christ returns to gather together the church, He will be announced by the voice of the archangel and the trump of God (1 Thess. 4:16-17). Believers will be clothed in a new body and the dead in Christ will be raised to receive a glorified body. From that moment we will enter into our rest—a glorious moment Paul referred to in Hebrews 4:9: "There remains a rest for God's people." This is the time when we will cease from our labors. This festival is also called a holy convocation.

The Hebrew word for "convocation" is *miqra* and alludes both to being "called out" and to a public gathering. A convocation is an appointed day to gather together with others for a specific spiritual gathering. Believers will be gathered from all nations and tongues in one location—the heavenly temple (Revelation 4 and 5).

Throughout history, the Feast of Trumpets has been given numerous names. Modern Jews mark this day as the first day of the secular calendar's Jewish New Year, called in Hebrew Rosh Hashanah, meaning "the head of the year." Trumpets is also called Yom Teruw'ah, *the day of the awakening blast*. Another name is Yom Hadin, referring to the *Day of Judgment*, and an unusual name, Yom HaZikaron, which is the *day of remembrance*. In Judaism, Trumpets is connected with three things: the Kingship of the Lord, the coronation of the King, and the resurrection of the just.

THE THREE TYPES OF TRUMPETS

It is interesting to see how these three types of trumpets fit into possible prophetic scenarios. The teruw'ah blast will be the awakening blast of the trump of God. It will awaken the dead in Christ, who shall rise first when Christ descends from heaven, and the living will be changed at the sound of the last trumpet (1 Cor. 15:52).

Since there is the sound of a *last* trump, there certainly is a blast from a *first* trump. The first blast is assigned to awaken the dead (who rise first) and the second blast (last trumpet) will change the bodies of the living. While most biblical trumpets are from animal horns, certain trumpets were beaten out of the precious metals of silver and gold. Moses identified these in Numbers 10, when he wrote of two silver trumpets that would be used for the calling of the congregation and for directing their movements. The first was a call to assemble the princes and heads of thousands. The second was a call to assemble the twelve tribes (Num. 10:3-5).

> "When they blow both of them, all of the congregation shall gather before you at the DOOR of the tabernacle of meeting."
> – Numbers 10:3 (NKJV)

Moses expressed a "prophetic revelation" in the second verse, which explains the two silver trumpets:

> "And the Lord spake unto Moses saying, Make thee two trumpets of silver; a whole piece shalt thou make them: that thou mayest use them for the calling of the assembly, and for the journeying of the camps."
> – Numbers 10:1 (KJV)

In the New Testament the Greek word for "church" is the *ekklesia*, which is a chosen assembly given special authority. The calling of the assembly (or the ekklesia) will occur for the church when the family of God in heaven and on Earth is united immediately after the trump of God sounds. They enter the door of heaven together (Rev. 4:1) and assemble at God's throne (Revelation 4 and 5). Notice the silver trumpets were used for the "journeying of the camps," or the journey of the twelve tribes. The church will make the journey to heaven following the blast of a trumpet. Then at the conclusion of the Tribulation, they will return to Earth as the armies of heaven (Rev. 19:14). We will swiftly travel from God's city to Earth, and as we enter the atmosphere, angels will be blowing trumpets to gather the elect from the four regions of the compass (Matt. 24:31).

In the wilderness, the silver trumpet was blown to draw the people from their tents to the door of God's presence. When John described being caught up in the Spirit into heaven, he saw a door in heaven and was thrust upward through the other side of the door. Both the living and the resurrected will be gathered together as they pass through a heavenly portal which ends at the sea of glass, the site of God's eternal throne (Rev. 4:1-6).

The idea of passing through a door or being behind a door is a theme throughout the Scriptures. The Ark of Noah had one door and when all things were prepared, God Himself shut the door (Gen. 7:16). In the parable of the wedding, a door was opened to allow the wise virgins to enter, and it was immediately closed to the five foolish virgins (Matt. 25:10). Once John moved in the Spirit from the island of Patmos through the heavenly portal, he stood immediately in heaven and saw the throne of God. The heavenly voice John heard saying "Come up hither" (Rev. 4:1) is interesting in light of the fact that Christ commanded, "Lazarus come forth," and spoke to a dead girl, commanding, "Damsel arise." In Revelation 11, the future two witnesses are slain by the Antichrist and will rise from the dead when they hear the heavenly voice say "Come up hither" (John 11:43; Mark 5:41; Rev. 11:12).

In these examples, the phrases *to arise, come up,* or *come forth* are all linked to someone being raised from the dead. When John was told to come up and see what would be hereafter, he was caught up just as believers will be caught up to meet the Lord in the air. The transition from the seven churches to the heavenly temple paints the imagery that the conclusion of the church age (Pentecost) will end at the sound of the voice and the trumpet (1 Thess. 4:16-17; Rev. 4:1-2).

THE SEVEN JERICHO TRUMPETS

Christ's Hebrew name is *Yeshua*, as is the Hebrew name translated as *Joshua* (Joshua 1:1). The eighty-five-year-old Joshua led the generation born in the wilderness into battle to capture the first Canaanite city called Jericho. This city was located at the entrance to the Promised Land and was fortified with massive stone walls. As per God's instructions, Joshua told the priests to march around the city seven times for six days and say nothing. On the seventh day (which was the end of the Festival of First Fruits), the seven priests were to take seven trumpets and march together seven times around the outer walls. The seventh time, they were to blow all seven trumpets at once to initiate a judgment against the city. This is when the walls fell and Israel entered the fortified city.

There is a striking parallel between the judgment of Jericho and the future Tribulation judgments on the cities of this world. In Revelation there are seven angels with seven trumpets and with each blast a specific natural or cosmic judgment is unleashed upon the earth. However, when the seventh angel blasts his trumpet, a major transition occurs:

> "But in the days of the voice of the seventh angel, when he shall begin to sound, the mystery of God should be finished, as he hath declared to his servants the prophets."
>
> – REV. 10:7 (KJV)

> "And the seventh angel sounded; and there were great voices in heaven, saying, the kingdoms of this world are become the kingdoms of our Lord, and of his Christ; and he shall reign forever and ever."
>
> – REV. 11:15 (KJV)

Just as the walls of Jericho fell on the seventh day with the seven blasts of trumpets and this city of Canaan became a first fruits city marked for Israel's promised inheritance, so the kingdoms of this world will collapse when the voice of the seventh angel sounds. At that moment, they will become the kingdoms of our God. The seventh angel will announce three woes, one of which will release an earthquake that destroys one-tenth of Jerusalem (Rev. 11:13).

REMEMBERING—MEMORIAL

An unusual Scripture penned by Malachi appears to connect with the Festival of Trumpets. As previously mentioned, rabbis consider the Feast of Trumpets to be a Day of Remembrance, noting that God marked it with the phrase, "a memorial of blowing of trumpets" (Lev.

23:24). The Hebrew word for memorial is *zikkaron*, which means to recall and bring something to mind, to mention, or to keep a written record. Malachi mentions a heavenly memorial book called the Book of Remembrance:

> "Then those who feared the Lord spoke to one another, and the Lord listened and heard them; So a book of remembrance was written before Him for those who fear the Lord and who med-itate on His name. They shall be Mine," says the Lord of hosts, on the day that I make them My jewels. And I will spare them as a man spares his own son who serves him."
>
> – MALACHI 3:16-17 (NKJV)

The Lord called the blowing of trumpets a memorial, or *zikkaron* of trumpets. The word for remembrance in Malachi 3:16 identifies this heavenly book as *zikkaron*. Thus this heavenly Book of Remembrance, mentioned only one time in Scripture, is linked to God *remembering someone for something done.* Notice that the names in this book are those who *fear God, meditate on His name,* and *speak (witness) to one another of the Lord.*

It must be noted that, in the context of Malachi (3:3-12), God is dealing with the Jews concerning their lack of giving tithe and offer-ings; thus this Book of Remembrance is also a marker where the names of givers to the kingdom are etched. One example of someone this book refers to is the centurion Cornelius, who feared God, gave much alms, and was praying when the angel of the Lord appeared in a vision and revealed to him that his prayers and alms (charity) had come up before God as a memorial (Acts 10:1-4). This word memorial in the Hebrew is *zikkaron*, meaning this man's name was in the Book of Remembrance and God was blessing him for his faithfulness.

In Malachi, however, the names in this book are sealed from the time of Tribulation coming upon the earth. Through Malachi, the Lord indicated that those whose names are recorded in the Book of Remembrance "will be mine when I make up my jewels." A promise of deliverance continues when God said, "I will spare them as a father does his son who serves him." The jewels are God's chosen, and to spare them would refer to sparing them from the coming Tribulation. This is clear when we continue to read, as Malachi 4 paints the imagery of the Tribulation. If God makes up His jewels and spares them from the Tribulation, then this is prophetic insight into the gathering together *prior* to the Tribulation.

YOM HAKESEH

A lesser known word connected to the Feast of Trumpets is Yom HaKeseh, which is "the Day of Hiding." The Hebrew root is *kacha*, which means "to conceal, cover and hide." All three fall festivals occur on the seventh Jewish month of Tishri. This month is preceded by the month of Elul, in which a shofar is blown for twenty-nine consecutive days, with the exception of the thirteenth day (in which there is silence) to remind the people that the day of Trumpets (Rosh Hashanah) is concealed in mystery. Psalms 81:3 refers to Rosh Hashanah (Trumpets) as we read, "Blow the trumpet in the new moon, in the time appointed, on our solemn feast day."

The secular Jewish New Year, called Rosh Hashanah, is also the Festival of Trumpets. The beginning of each Jewish month is marked with the new moon and not a full moon. Each month begins in darkness, but the first day is when the shining sliver of the moon is spotted. Passover is always celebrated during a full moon, along with Tabernacles. However, at Trumpets the moon is concealed, which to me signifies that the world is preparing to enter the darkness of the Tribulation!

Just as the blast of trumpets at Jericho signaled Israel's transition, the memorial of blowing of trumpets is a transition from the believer's Passover redemption to the world's Atonement judgments, designed to purge the wicked nations and prepare the Jewish remnant for the rule of the King-Messiah. Thus, Trumpets is a transitional festival. This is why it has no Old Testament or New Testament parallels except for the rapture. Just as there is a mystery that surrounds this particular day, Paul wrote about the mystery of the resurrection:

"Behold I shew you a mystery; We shall not all sleep, but we shall be changed, in a moment, in the twinkling of an eye, at the last trump: for the trumpet shall sound..."

– 1 CORINTHIANS 15:52 (KJV)

Infants are concealed in their mother's womb until the very moment of their birth. Only when the pregnant mother experiences birth pains can she know that the child who has been *concealed* will soon be *revealed*. Christ used this metaphor of birth pains when listing the signs of His coming: wars, rumors of war, famines, pestilence, and earthquakes in different places (Matt. 24:6-7). He said, "All these are the beginning of sorrows." (The Greek word for "sorrows" means *birth pangs* – Matt. 24:8). The global birth pangs listed in Christ's Olivet discourse are the early indicators that the concealed Messiah will soon become the revealed Messiah.

Isaac's wife Rebekah, after nineteen years of barrenness, became pregnant with twins. According to the Annals of World History, from the time of creation to the year the twins wrestled within her womb, was 2,167 years. Two nations were brought forth: Jacob, the father of Israel's twelve tribes, and Esau, the father of the Edomites. The twins struggled in the birth process to determine who would be the first born. The firstborn received both a blessing and a birthright among the ancients (see Gen. 27:36).

After the painful *travail* of the holocaust, the descendants of Jacob were reborn as a nation on May 14, 1948, thus fulfilling Isaiah's prediction that a nation would be born at once: "For as soon as Zion travailed, she brought forth her children" (Isa. 66:8). From 1948 to 1967, Jerusalem was divided between two nations—Jordan and Israel, or historically the sons of Esau and the sons of Jacob. Then in 1967, Jerusalem, the original home of the first king and priest Melchizedek, was reunited as the capital of Israel following a six-day war. The only other six-day war in Israel's history was the battle of Jericho.

These two dates, 1948 and 1967, set two ancient families, two sons and their cousins, wrestling for their position in a land inheritance. From a spiritual view, Esau's descendants desire to have back their birthright which the patriarch of the family sold for a bowl of soup (Gen. 25:32-34).

CLUES TO THE DAY AND THE HOUR

There is a nugget concealed in the statement that Christ made concerning His return, and I believe it is connected with Yom HaKeseh.

> "But of that day and hour knows no man, no, not the angels of heaven, but my Father only."
>
> – MATTHEW 24:36 (KJV)

Before and after the time of Christ, the Feast of Trumpets was the only festival of the seven in which the exact day it was to begin was not known. The reason was because this feast begins on the first day of a new month, and the beginning of the month was not marked by a paper calendar. It was marked by the first sighting of the moon. In ancient times, a forty-eight-hour window was established to give time for two witnesses to testify before the high priest and Sanhedrin that the moon had been "sanctified." Thus, no man knew the exact day or hour when the first trumpet on the festival would be sounded.

A visible manifestation of the moon was a sign that the festival was beginning. Likewise, Jesus told us there would be cosmic signs, including signs in the moon, prior to His return (Luke 21:25-26; Joel 2:30-31). The world observed the four blood moons that occurred on the first days of Passover and the first days of Tabernacles, in both 2014 and 2015. Prophetic students considered this a sign of Joel's prophecy about the moon becoming blood before the great and terrible day of the Lord.

Just as the moon was concealed and the day of the trumpets was unknown until a cosmic sign was seen, so also is the day and hour of Christ's return unknown; but cosmic signs will precede that moment. When the disciples asked Christ, "Will you at this time restore the kingdom to Israel?" (Acts 1:6), Christ responded, "It is not for you to know the times or the seasons..." (Acts 1:7). From a Hebraic perspective, the word *seasons* would be an allusion to the appointed seasons— that is, the seven festivals. The word *times* in Greek is *chronos*, which refers to a specific time that is set on the linear timeline, a set space of time in which God has predetermined an event. Christ gave this statement around AD 32 or 33.

Many years later, Saul of Tarsus converted to Christ and became the Apostle Paul. After Paul received the revelation of Christ's return for the church (1 Thess. 4:16-17), he wrote: "Of the times and seasons, brethren, you have no need I write to you. For you yourselves know perfectly well that the day of the Lord so comes as a thief in the night" (1 Thess. 5:1-2). With the completion of the New Testament and the apocalyptic vision of John written in the book of Revelation, we now have a better understanding of the times and seasons.

With Christ's emphasis on cosmic activity including signs in the moon, we must discern not just the cycles of the past blood moons, but understand the connection of the moon being concealed prior to the Feast of Trumpets. Since nobody knew the exact day or hour of the moon's reappearance, and no man knows the day or hour of Christ's return, the link between these two truths and the Feast of Trumpets is undeniable.

CHAPTER 8

DOES ONE GENERATION REMAIN FOR THE END TO COME?

ONE OF THE most misunderstood, yet commonly quoted verses related to the events and timing of Christ's return is found in Matthew 24, where Christ answered a question from His disciples. The verse has been a source of controversy in our time.

First, some background. Christ was on the Mount of Olives, a large hill positioned outside the Eastern Gate in Jerusalem. Zechariah predicted that the Lord's feet will one day stand on this mountain and initiate an earthquake that will split the mountain in two halves (Zech. 14:1-8). On that day the Lord will be proclaimed King. With this in mind, the disciples were admiring the beautiful stones of the Jewish temple, as one could sit on top of the Mount of Olives, peer over Jerusalem's stone wall, and see the temple compound and its bright, white stone and gold crown adorning the roof.

Jesus interrupted the moment by warning that the buildings and walls they were admiring would be destroyed in the future and that "not one stone shall be left here upon another, that shall not be thrown down" (Matt. 24:2). The disciples understood that Daniel had predicted trouble at the time of the end (Dan. 8:17; 11:35, 40; 12:4, 9). The Jewish Messiah was thought to be a victor over Israel's political enemies. Thus the disciples perhaps were confused that, if Christ were the Messiah, why would He not protect the temple? They must have thought that this destruction was connected to Daniel's time of the end (Dan. 11:35, 40; 12:4, 9).

This unexpected warning sparked three important questions from Christ's disciples, as found in Matthew 24:3:

1. When shall these things shall be (referring to the destruction of the temple)?

2. What will be the sign of your coming (referring to His return to the Mount of Olives)?

3. What will be the sign of the end of the world (literally end of the age)?

Jesus answered by warning of wars, rumors of wars, famines, pestilences, and earthquakes in different places. When these combined events are witnessed, He said this would be the beginning of sorrows (Matt. 24:8). The Greek word for sorrows is *odin*, and literally refers to *birth pains*. God often uses a natural example to express a spiritual truth. In the Old Testament, the severe trouble and trials Israel experienced which broke their pride and humbled them were compared to birth pains and a woman in travail (Psa. 48:6; Jer. 6:24; Mic. 4:10). Christ also used this analogy when He forewarned His disciples of His suffering, and compared it to a woman who experiences great labor pains but forgets her agony once the child has been born (John 16:20-21).

A pregnancy is divided into three trimesters—the first, second, and third—counting from conception to birth at the end of the ninth month. The most severe pains occur in the hours before the birth. In the Matthew 24 discourse, three distinct questions dealt with the destruction of the temple, the signs of His coming, and the signs of the end of the age. As Christ laid out a prophetic timeline, He divided

His discourse into three sections. The wars, rumors of wars, famines, pestilence, and earthquakes were actually part of the years leading up to the destruction of the temple. The Jewish historian Josephus wrote about the wars of the Jews. He revealed the massive slaughter of Jews who fled from the Romans and the civil wars that broke out. The famines were so bad in Judea that many died and others boiled shoe leather and attempted to eat it.

Some interpret the word earthquakes as political and social upheavals and commotions. However, the word is literally a physical shaking of land. According to Josephus, prior to the destruction of Jerusalem in AD 70, several earthquakes occurred throughout the Roman Empire. Strange cosmic activity was observed in Jerusalem as a star hung over the city like a sword, and a comet was seen for one whole year. At the Festival of Unleavened Bread during the ninth hour of the night, a great light shone on the altar and the temple, continuing to shine for about an hour. Before sunset, people all over the country reported seeing chariots and armies fighting in the clouds and besieging cities *(source: Josephus, Antiquities of the Jews)*. In Matthew 24:3-8, Christ listed the signs that would occur prior to the destruction of the temple, signs that will also be repeated prior to His return.

Christ made it clear that when these events occur, the end is not yet—meaning the end of the age which would lead to His return to Earth (Matt. 24:6). These were the beginning of sorrows, or birth pains (24:8). In prophetic terms, I call these the first trimester of prophetic signs.

Christ did not stop there with His predictions. He continued to warn of hatred against believers, and that Israel would be hated above all nations. Then He predicted betrayals and offenses, with iniquity abounding and love growing cold. False prophets would rise and great deception would follow. These predictions are certainly being fulfilled in our own time! Christ summed up this section (verses 9-13) with this statement:

> "And this gospel of the kingdom shall be preached in all the world for a witness unto all nations; and then shall the end come."
>
> – Matthew 24:14 (KJV)

The Gospel was preached for forty years throughout the Roman Empire, and by the time of Jerusalem's destruction in AD 70, the message had spread into Asia Major, Asia Minor, Northern Africa, and Europe. Christianity was on the move and Christians were being heavily persecuted by Nero and other Roman Emperors who followed him. The temple and Jerusalem were destroyed by the Roman tenth legion. But the Gospel continued and still continues to this day, as Christianity has grown from a million followers in the first century to over two billion today.

In Matthew 24:15, Christ moved forward in time and alluded to an abomination that will make Jerusalem desolate. This abomination is first mentioned in Daniel 11:31 and 12:11. Some suggest this abomination occurred in 168 BC when Antiochus Epiphanes invaded Jerusalem and offered a pig on the brass altar for his god Zeus. However, this is not what Christ was referring to, as indicated by Matthew admitting he did not understand this statement:

> "When ye therefore shall see the abomination of desolation, spoken by Daniel the prophet, stand in the holy place (whoso readeth, let him understand)."
>
> – MATT. 24:15 (KJV)

If this abomination had *already occurred*, then why would Christ have predicted this as a future event, and why would Matthew confess he was uncertain of the meaning of Christ's warning? Some older Bible scholars say that this abomination occurred when the Roman army besieged Jerusalem and brought the Roman standards (metal eagles, which were the Roman ensign) onto the Temple Mount against the eastern gate and sacrificed to them. However, many years after Matthew penned this narrative, and twenty-five years after the temple was destroyed, John wrote Revelation and revealed a time when the false prophet would make an image to the Antichrist in Jerusalem and cause the image to speak and live through demonic power. Those who do not worship the image will be killed (Rev. 13:11-18). In the context of the abomination warning, note that (in verse 15) Jesus moved forward in time to the signs of the Tribulation and the end of the age. Thus the abomination that Daniel predicts occurs during the Tribulation.

The third trimester pangs that are the most severe are the seasons of the Great Tribulation (Matt. 24:21) that will conclude with the return of Christ to the Mount of Olives (Zech. 14:4; Rev. 19:11-16). Christ warned that in those days (at the time of the abomination in Jerusalem) those living in the city (Jerusalem) and Judea should flee out of the area to the mountain. He warned that this abomination would unleash a false Christ performing signs and wonders that would deceive multitudes.

The Apostle John revealed that in the Great Tribulation a false prophet will arise who will demonstrate amazing signs and wonders. For example, he will create an image (the Greek word is *icon*), make it live, and call fire down from heaven. These satanically-inspired signs will deceive entire nations into following the Antichrist (Rev. 13:11-18).

There will be a Jewish remnant, however, that will flee into the wilderness for forty-two months, where God will protect them and prevent the Antichrist or his armies from slaying this remnant (see Revelation 12). Matthew 24:16-20 fits with John's writings of the Jewish persecution during the future Tribulation.

At the same time, scholars note that several years prior to the destruction of the temple in AD 70, a large population of believers recalled the words of Jesus when He warned to flee the city when you see Jerusalem surrounded by armies (Luke 21:20-21). During a brief break in the siege, Christians rejected the idea of rebelling against the Roman occupiers, and instead chose to flee to the mountains in Jordan to an area called Pella, where they received asylum and built a Christian community.

The fact that these passages refer to both an event in the past and events in the future brings forth the possibility that Christ might have been making parallel predictions that refer to His generation as well as a final generation that will experience the same signs. This is possible since He refers to the past narratives of the days of Noah and Lot, and says they will repeat themselves in the future (see Luke 17:26-32).

Christ continued His warning of horrific cosmic signs, falling stars, and the powers of heaven being shaken (Matt. 24:29). These cosmic harbingers will be the climax of the Tribulation and then the "sign of the Son of Man" will appear in heaven (Matt. 24:30). This appearing is not the catching away and resurrection of the dead in Christ, mentioned in 1 Thessalonians 4:16-17; it is the appearing to set up Christ's Messianic Kingdom in Jerusalem where He will rule for a thousand years (Rev. 20:4).

THE GENERATIONAL CONFUSION

After Christ explained the signs of the temple's destruction, His coming, and the end of the age, He made one statement that has been the primary source of predicting dates for His return:

> "Now learn this parable from the fig tree: When its branch has already become tender and puts forth leaves, you know that summer is near. So you also, when you see all these things, know it is near – at the doors! Assuredly, I say to you, this generation will by no means pass away, till all these things take place."
>
> – MATTHEW 24:32-34 (NKJV)

Genea is the Greek word for generation, which can have several meanings. It can refer to people of the same lineage, such as an ancestral family; a race of people with the same ethnic background or nationality; a specific age; or a multitude of people who all lived at the same moment in history. When Christ said that this generation shall not pass, some suggest He was referring to those from His generation who would see these signs appear. The weakness of this interpretation is that Christ's generation (within thirty-eight years) saw portions of Matthew 24 fulfilled, but did not see the false prophets, counterfeit miracles, dangerous cosmic signs, the sign of the Son of Man in the heavens, or the angels returning to collect the remnant of Jews and bring them to Jerusalem.

The second view is that the word generation here simply refers to the Jewish race that would not perish from the earth, but be living at the time when all these signs occur. The third view teaches that there is a specific timeframe in which these events will all be fulfilled.

The controversy that some groups suggest has been that all of Matthew 24, from the signs of the destruction to the time of Great Tribulation, refers to the years leading up to the destruction of the temple. Others believe that, with the exception of the temple signs, none of Matthew 24 has yet occurred, but will be fulfilled during the future Tribulation. In reality, the truth lies in the middle.

The confusion can be settled when we realize how the prophets and seers of the Scripture viewed the future. Prophets such as Isaiah would write about their present condition, and then suddenly jump far into the future to give insight about the day when Messiah would be on Earth, then be pulled back into their time to complete their warnings. In Revelation, John is caught up in the Spirit into heaven (Rev. 4:1-2) and views the future from a heavenly vantage point. One moment he describes the heavenly throne room, and moments later he sees something unfold on Earth, then he is standing at the Heavenly Temple, when suddenly he sees caverns open under the earth (Revelation 9). The book is one long narrative from three different views: events in heaven, events on Earth, and events under the earth.

In prophecy, the first rule of interpretation is to take the words at their primary, ordinary, and literal meaning, unless there is apocalyptic symbolism or parables used that require interpretation using other scriptures.

The best examples of a double reference are found in the Psalms. The Apostle Peter called David a prophet (Acts 2:29-30) and the Psalms are replete with statements related to David's personal life, yet they are clearly a double reference to himself and the Messiah. For example:

> "For thou wilt not leave my soul in hell; neither wilt thou suffer thine Holy One to see corruption."
>
> – PSALM 16:10 (KJV)

At Pentecost, Peter quoted this exact passage to the large Jewish audience and related it as a prophecy of Christ's death and resurrection, as Christ's body never saw corruption and God brought Him out of the grave (Acts 2:27). Another example is found in Ezekiel 28, where the prophet chronicles the wealth, power, and pride of the earthly king of Tyre. Yet, in the middle of his narrative, the scene changes to that of an anointed cherub who once walked upon the holy mountain in the midst of stones of fire, and who is brought down because of his pride. These references are not, as some teach, a metaphor or allegory referring to the earthly king of Tyre. They do, however, fall into the category of double reference.

To correctly interpret Matthew 24, one must understand the double reference. Jesus spoke to His generation and later in the discourse switched forward to the time of the end to a final generation that would be living at His return to Earth. Understanding this can keep a person from concluding that all of Matthew 24 had to be fulfilled in the first century, prior to AD 70. The truth is that the final, end-time generation will experience the same signs that first century Israel saw: wars, rumors of wars, famines, pestilences, and so forth.

The difference is that these signs in the first century were spread out over a period of years and eventually climaxed at Jerusalem, where both the temple and the city were destroyed on the 9th of Av on the Jewish calendar. Matthew said "All of these are the beginning of sorrows" (birth pains, see Matt. 24:8). "All of these" can refer to all of these events combined or coming together at once, thus occurring at the same time. We are the generation that is literally seeing all of these things occur at once. In one day we can hear of a war or a rumor of war, a famine, or an earthquake somewhere in the world. New plagues and deadly diseases strike the world. Luke spoke of these same signs and said, "When these things begin to happen, look up and lift up your heads, because your redemption draws near" (Luke 21:28).

Jesus gave signs to *His generation* and to a *future generation*. The next prophetic dispute involves the meaning of the word generation. Many students of prophecy mark a generation as a specific time period. In the Old Testament the length of a generation varied, as prior to Noah's flood man lived hundreds of years. Methuselah lived to be 969, while Enoch lived 365 years. After the flood, the lifespan for the average man was reduced to fewer than two hundred years. Abraham lived to be 175 (Gen. 25:7) and Moses lived 120 years (Deut 34:7). In the time of the Exodus, Moses wrote that a person can live seventy years, and by reason of strength up to eighty years (Psa. 90:10). The reduction in the length of a generation is linked to the reduction in the years of a man's life. After the flood, the average man was thirty-six years of age when his first son was born. Moses, however, spoke of the Israelites in the wilderness provoking God for forty years, and said God was grieved with that *generation*—meaning *all of the people* who came out of Egypt. This generation who had unbelief died in the wilderness within forty years.

Christ warned His own generation that the judgment of shedding innocent blood from Abel to Zechariah would come upon His generation (Matt. 23:34-39). At Christ's judgment before Pilate, the religious leaders cried out, "His blood be upon us and on our children" (Matt. 27:25). Christ gave this prediction between AD 30 to 32, and the fulfillment of the judgment upon Jerusalem came to complete fruition in AD 70, which would have been thirty-eight to forty years after it was spoken.

When Christ said this generation shall not pass until all is fulfilled, this would include the Gospel being preached around the world, the abomination that makes Jerusalem desolate, the cosmic harbingers, and His return to Earth at the conclusion of the Great Tribulation. This implies that there will be one generation, a specific group of people at a specific time, who will witnesses all these signs of His coming, indicating the end of the age.

In prophecy or Scripture, it is easy to identify the length of a generation, especially when comparing narratives, Scriptures, and history. But what is the starting point when determining the length of that generation?

Some begin the final generation in 1948 when Israel was restored as a nation. Others note that Jerusalem is the key to all end-time prophecy and the trigger date for the last generation would be 1967, when Israel reunited Jerusalem as the capital of Israel after the six-day war (see Psalms 102:16). Others believe the timing, just as it was during the Exodus, is centered more on the Jewish people returning from the four corners of the earth back to Israel, which could begin in the late 1980s, when Russian Jews were released to return to Israel. Still others attempt to base the time of the final generation on certain signs, such as cosmic activity or treaties being signed in Israel.

I believe it is futile to time a specific generation or the length thereof for several reasons. First, where does the starting point for the cycle begin? In 1948, when Israel was restored as a nation? In 1967, when Jerusalem was reunited? During cosmic signs, such as the blood moon cycles of 2014 and 2015? Second, how long is a generation? Is it forty years? Fifty years, seventy years, or a hundred years?

Never lose sight of the main point. There is a generation of people that will see the signs, experience the birth pangs, and be alive when Christ returns for the true believers and to resurrect the dead in Christ. Thus, we should live daily, not with anxiety, but with anticipation that the Messiah will return just as He promised.

CHAPTER 9

PARALLEL SIGNS OF THE FIRST AND SECOND COMING

FOR MANY YEARS I have taught a spiritual principle understood by King Solomon: "That which has been is that which shall be..." (Eccl. 1:9-10). History is cyclical and events tend to repeat themselves, especially events that impact nations and the world.

The Bible is filled with examples of cycles and repetitive events. First, consider that God Himself established festivals, seven in all, that are repeated yearly, on the same day of the same month, with the same rituals, harvest cycles, and celebration patterns. Every seventh year, God established a year of rest for the land, animals, and farmers, called the Shemitah. The Jubilee cycle occurred every fiftieth year, and the weekly Shabbat (Sabbath) was always on the seventh day, from sunset on Friday until sunset on Saturday. These festivals, new moons, and sabbatical cycles were set at the same times and seasons.

Historical narratives are also repeated. The first Passover at the time of the Exodus (see Exod. 12) was a preview of the crucifixion of Christ near Passover (Mark 14:1). Christ resurrected and showed Himself alive to His disciples during the time of the Feast of First Fruits, which represented offering to God the first fruits of the barley harvest. The giving of the Law on Mount Sinai, fifty days after the Exodus, would be a preview of the Day of Pentecost, the outpouring of the Holy Spirit, and the birth of the church in Acts 2:1-4. The three fall festivals—Trumpets, Atonement and Tabernacles—will have their complete fulfillment in the future with the rapture, the Tribulation, and the millennial Kingdom of Christ.

In early history a righteous man named Enoch lived 365 years and was supernaturally translated to heaven (Gen. 5:23-24; Heb. 11:5). Enoch, the seventh from Adam, gives believers a preview of those who will be changed and caught up to meet the Lord in the air at His coming (1 Thess. 4:16-17). In Genesis 11, we read of a high tower called Babel being built, which was going to be the first global government and "new world order." But God demolished it and confused the people's languages. In Revelation 17 and 18, at the end of days we read of a "mystery Babylon" that will exist, which God will destroy. History repeats itself, and repetitive cycles are evident in both secular and religious history.

Compare the parallels of events today with some of the events and global circumstances at the time of Christ's birth.

1. THE ANTICIPATION OF THE MESSIAH

Near the time of the birth of Christ, there was an expectation that Israel was on the verge of the unveiling of their Messiah. This is evident from several narratives.

Shortly after Christ was born in Bethlehem, the holy family, being from the house of David and the tribe of Judah, journeyed about eight miles to the holy temple in Jerusalem, where they were greeted by an aged rabbi named Simeon. Based on a spiritual revelation, Simeon was informed by the Holy Spirit that he would not die until he saw the Lord's Christ, meaning the Messiah of Israel, sent from God (Luke 2:26). After blessing the infant Christ and releasing a prophetic word to Mary concerning her son's future, the rabbi looked up and told God that now he would depart this life in peace, as his eye had seen the salvation of Israel (Luke 2:29-30).

The second senior citizen to recognize this newborn infant as the Messiah of Israel was an eighty-four-year-old widow, a prophetess named Anna, who served God continually in fasting and prayer.

When she overheard Simeon's prophecies and saw the child, she openly began to speak of Him to all who were looking for the redemption in Jerusalem (Luke 2:36-38). Both of these godly individuals were given supernatural revelation by the Holy Spirit that this child was the Messiah, and that He had arrived in Israel. These older believers were discerning of the times and knew that the four-thousand-year-old prophecy (that the seed of the woman would crush the head of the serpent) given by God in Eden just after the Fall was now in its early stages (see Gen. 3:15).

TODAY'S PROPHETIC PARALLEL

In all my years of ministry, I have never seen such a high level of anticipation concerning the possibility of Christ's imminent return. Like Simeon and Anna, there is an older mature generation that has great discernment of the times. There is a generation that will be alive on Earth and who will, as Enoch did, escape death and experience the glorious return of Christ for the church. Simeon waited, perhaps wondering every day if this could be the day of His arrival. Finally, his expectations were fulfilled when he held Christ in his arms. There is one generation, consisting of all ages, that will not face death but will be alive, changed in a moment and caught up to meet the Lord in the air when He returns (1 Thess. 4:16-17; 1 Cor. 15:51-52).

2. STRANGE COSMIC HARBINGERS

Simeon and Anna understood the birth by spiritual revelation, but the next group that came from a long distance to celebrate the arrival of the Messiah were wise men (called Magi) who had seen a strange cosmic harbinger in the sky—a star. They followed it to Israel, to Judea, and finally to Bethlehem where they visited Christ in a house (Matt. 2:1-11). What was this star? It might have been a new star that just appeared, an alignment of planets, or a comet. We can only speculate. However, we know for certain that cosmic signs were a part of the birth of the Messiah.

Today's Prophetic Parallel

Just prior to Christ's return, "there will be signs in the sun, the moon, and the stars" (Luke 21:25). The final generation will understand these cosmic signs and use them to discern the times. Such signs can include, but are not limited to, solar and lunar eclipses falling on Jewish festivals, solar flares, asteroids and meteorites, and fearful and great signs in the heavens that are revealed through telescopes and satellites.

3. THE WORLD WAS BEING TAXED

The economic situation at that time is also interesting. The Roman armies were occupying many lands, including Palestine and Jerusalem. Prior to Christ's birth, a decree came from Caesar Augustus that all the world should be taxed (Luke 2:1). The 750th anniversary of the birth of Rome was occurring about the time of Christ's birth, and Augustus had planned major celebrations throughout the Roman Empire. It has been suggested that the entire empire was taxed to help pay for this huge government-sponsored celebration.

Today's Prophetic Parallel

The debt, spending, and borrowing in nations, including the United States, are out of control. The spending is unsustainable and the borrowing so high that it cannot be paid back. The only solution known to politicians is to raising tax revenues. In the United States, everything we purchase is taxed—food, gas, clothing, cars, property, utilities, phones, etc.. Those living in Christ's time bore economic responsibilities, just as today the middle class bears the brunt of the economic tax burden.

4. INFANTS WERE BEING SLAUGHTERED

Herod, one of the governors in the area of Judea, became fearful of the new infant who was born "King of the Jews." He issued a decree for the Roman soldiers to kill all male children under two years of age, not just in Bethlehem, but in surrounding villages (Matt. 2:16). Many scholars believe this would have covered about a ten-mile radius. This was a government instituted "after-birth abortion." The lives of infants meant nothing to the hard-hearted government leader and the calloused Roman soldiers.

TODAY'S PROPHETIC PARALLELS

The numbers of abortions performed in America exceed the number of American soldiers who died in every war America has fought since its inception. When an infant dies from being forcibly removed from the mother's womb, this becomes the sin of the shedding innocent blood, which is one of the seven sins that God hates (Prov. 6:17). According to the words of Christ, Jerusalem's destruction (which occurred in AD 70) was a result of the Jewish leaders shedding the blood of the prophets and the righteous men. Christ mentioned that the religious leaders slew Zechariah between the porch and the altar (Matt. 23:35). God remembers when innocent blood is shed, and the voice concealed within the blood of a victim can cry out from the ground (see Gen. 4:10). Eventually, God severely judges those who shed the blood of the innocent (see Rev. 6:10 and 17:6-16).

Many of the same events occurring at Christ's first appearing are repeating themselves as we draw closer to His next appearing. I call this the "double signs of prophetic seasons." Prophecy tends to move forward on a horizontal timeline. The patterns can become repetitive, similar to starting at one point and moving clockwise in a circle, until you come back to the starting point. Much can be learned by observing previous patterns of prophetic history, knowing that it tends to come back around at some point. For example, we can expect the patterns of Christ's first appearance during the Roman Empire period to repeat themselves in the time of His second coming, with national governments moving from sovereign entities to global coalitions.

CHAPTER 10

TRIGGERS TO THE TRIBULATION

Two important words in the New Testament must be understood in order to discover the triggers that release the future Great Tribulation: times and seasons. When the disciples asked Christ if He was preparing to restore the kingdom to Israel, He responded, "It is not for you to know the times or the seasons which the Father has put in His own power" (Acts 1:7). The Greek word for times is *kairos*, and can refer to an opportune time, or a time when things come to a head, as *kairos* comes from *kara*, meaning "head". The same word is translated in Acts 1:7 for "seasons".

Among the ancients, two words were used to distinguish time. One was *chronos* and the other *kairos*. Chronos refers to an orderly chronological sequence of events or time. There are different interpretations for kairos time; however, it refers more to events over time that come to a point. We could say it means the climax of time. It would take ample space to review the philosophical meanings of these words as written by thinkers such as Aristotle, or the teachings of Christ and Paul, who also spoke of times and seasons (1 Thess. 5:1). However, there is a sequence of predicted events that begin to occur at the same time and which initiate a response. In this case, signs of the times begin to collide with one another at a specific time and initiate the last days based upon the fulfillment of certain predetermined signs recorded by the biblical prophets.

When the word "seasons" is used, the rabbinical and Hebraic thought differ somewhat from Greek thought. Among the devout Jews, the seasons are connected to the seasons of God, or the seven major festivals that are set times on the Hebrew calendar: Passover, Unleavened Bread, First Fruits, Pentecost, Trumpets, Atonement, and Tabernacles. When Christ spoke of the "season which God has put in His own power," He was referring to the prophetic events spoken of among the Hebrew prophets of Scripture that predicted the reign of the Messiah on Earth as King of kings from His throne in Jerusalem. Only God Himself controls the prediction and fulfillment of prophecy. Even Christ said that neither He or the angels, but only the Father in heaven, knows the day and hour that He will return to Earth (Matt. 24:36).

The fact that seasons or Jewish festivals, also called "the time appointed" (Exod. 23:15), are linked with the seven yearly festivals indicates that God moves in an orderly fashion and at set seasons which He appointed. The months themselves may vary slightly, as the Hebrew lunisolar calendar has 354/355 days, compared to the 365/366 day solar calendar. The Jewish month actually began when the first evidence of the moon was observed by two witnesses, who then reported their sighting to the Sanhedrin in Jerusalem, and was then confirmed to the high priest. Passover was always during a full moon, along with Tabernacles. The one festival in which no one knew the exact day and hour was Trumpets, which began when the white sliver of the moon was spotted, marking the time as the first day (of the seventh month).

There is significance to times and season. When we study the biblical concept of the "fullness of times," much can be found in the prophetic Scriptures related to the return of the Messiah and His future kingdom. One very significant passage is in Ephesians:

> "That in the dispensation of the fullness of the times He might gather together in one all things in Christ, both which are in heaven and which are on earth—in Him."
>
> – Eph. 1:10 (NKJV)

The word "dispensation" is used four times by Paul, in 1 Corinthians 9:17, Ephesians 1:10 and 3:2, and Colossians 1:25 (KJV). Paul spoke of the "dispensation of the Gospel" (1 Cor. 9:17) and "the dispensation of the grace of God" (Eph. 3:2). Some theologians dislike the word dispensation, especially those who disagree with the dispensational teaching that God has divided the history of mankind, from Adam to the present, into several timeframes where a particular characteristic marked that particular period. For example, Adam living in the Garden of Eden was "the dispensation of innocence". From the Fall to the flood of Noah was "the dispensation of conscience". After the flood of Noah we see the formation of government (the tower of Babel), which initiated "the dispensation of human government". With the promises given to Abraham and his descendants, "the dispensation of promise" was initiated. Christ, through the New Covenant, gave mankind "the dispensation of grace". The Apostle Paul called this the "dispensation of the grace of God" (Eph. 3:2).

The Greek word "dispensation" has a rich meaning. The word is *oikonomia*, and it refers to the management of a house or an estate. It means to be a steward over the affairs of a wealthy individual. In this context, the body of believers on Earth oversees the preaching, teaching, and administration of the Gospel message of grace, ensuring that the teachings of Christ remain pure and without corruption.

THE FULLNESS OF TIMES

There is a "dispensation of the fullness of times". The word "times" (plural) indicates several different types of fullness that will occur during the same timeframe. One is the fullness of the preaching of the Gospel around the world, and at completion the end will come (Matt. 24:14). Another is "the fullness of iniquity", when transgression reaches a peak (see Dan. 8:23). A third fullness (when "the times of the Gentiles are fulfilled") occurs when full control of Jerusalem is removed from Gentile empires and the Jewish people have complete political and economic control over the city (Luke 21:24). When referring to the fullness of something, it can be linked to different situations.

THE WORD OF THE LORD FROM ZION

That which has been will be, and that which has been done shall be done in the future. On the Feast of Pentecost, the Gospel message supernaturally birthed the Christian church (Acts 2:1-4). From Jerusalem the Gospel spread to Judea, Samaria, and eventually the uttermost parts of the earth (Acts 1:8). With the destruction of Jerusalem in AD 70, Rome, Italy eventually became the center for Christianity.

Since prophetic time flows cyclically, then the Gospel at the time of the end will spread around the world, with the final flame of the Gospel centering in Jerusalem, near the mountains of Zion. Today, not far from the three ancient, sacred hills of Ophel, Zion, and Moriah are two Christian television networks, Daystar and TBN, which carry the word of the Lord from Jerusalem to the nations!

THE TRIGGER TO RELEASE THE TRIBULATION

I have often pondered what the primary trigger will be that will activate the final Tribulation on Earth. I believe the answer is summed up in this phrase: men will no longer repent. Consider the days of Noah, Lot, and the time of Christ. Noah was called a preacher of righteousness (2 Peter 2:5). He warned his generation of the coming deluge, yet nobody outside of his immediate family responded to his message. Thus, nobody repented. After Lot was warned by two angels, he ran to the homes of his married daughters and warned them to get out of the city. Lot's words fell on deaf ears, and the sons-in-law thought Lot was joking. Sodom was so corrupt that the people did not even consider repenting of their sins. Nobody repented before God sent fire and turned four cities of the plain into ashes (Gen. 19:14-29).

Then there were the days of Christ. This was an odd generation, as they saw miracles, including the raising of the dead; yet many religious Pharisees and Sadducees refused to believe Christ was the promised Messiah. Christ said that if the same miracles had been done in Sodom, the people would have repented and the city would have remained until Christ's day (Matt. 11:23). He warned that destruction would strike Jerusalem in one generation as the city was guilty before

God for shedding the innocent blood of prophets, including an Old Testament prophet, Zechariah, whom temple priests slew between the porch and the altar (2 Chron. 24:20-21; Matt. 23:35-36). When Pilate washed his hands and declared Christ innocent, and the religious multitude proclaimed, "His blood be upon us and our children" (Matt 27:25), it was thirty-eight years later when Jerusalem was surrounded by Roman armies and the temple destroyed. This fulfilled the warning of Jesus that the temple would be destroyed (Matt. 24:1-3).

WHEN MEN NO LONGER REPENT

Mercy is always released to those who humble themselves and repent before God. However, there have been seasons in Israel's history when the people became spiritually blind and worshipped idols, turning from God's commandments and refusing to correct the error of their ways. In Israel's early history, this led to an open door for Israel's enemies to take the people into captivity (see the book of Judges).

John notes in the book of Revelation that, despite judgments that take out a third of the global population and leave billions victim to the kingdom of the beast, people refuse to repent during the Tribulation. "They blasphemed the God of heaven because of their pains and their sores, and repented not of their deeds" (Rev. 16:11).

It seems that lack of repentance could be the trigger that ends the church age and begins the Tribulation. The assignment of the church is to preach the gospel throughout the world for a witness to all nations; and then the end shall come (Matt. 24:14). People are instructed to repent and be baptized (Acts 2:38). When people begin to harden their hearts to the gospel and refuse to listen or repent, there is no longer a need for God to release mercy and grace. It will be time to unleash the judgments spoken of by biblical prophets. Paul wrote:

> "But in accordance with your hardness and your impenitent heart you are treasuring up for yourself wrath in the day of wrath and revelation of the righteous judgment of God, who "will render to each one according to his deeds": eternal life to those who by patient continuance in doing good seek for glory, honor, and immortality; but to those who are self-seeking and do not obey

the truth, but obey unrighteousness--indignation and wrath, tribulation and anguish, on every soul of man who does evil..."

– ROMANS 2:5-9 (NKJV)

As long as men will turn to the true God, repent of their wickedness, and have their lives transformed by the Gospel, the dispensation of grace will continue. But at some point, people will reject the Gospel, ignore warnings, and walk in the hardness of their hearts. When this occurs, the Tribulation is soon to arrive.

CHAPTER 11

THE TERMINATION OF
THE CHURCH AGE

THE FINAL BOOK of the Bible is Revelation, called "The Apocalypse" (apokalupsis in Greek). The book can be divided into the things that were, that are (at the moment John saw the vision), and that shall be (in the future). The first three chapters are a specific word for seven churches, all of which existed in John's time. Each church is personally addressed with a message concerning their strengths or weaknesses, a commendation or a warning, and a future blessing promised for them if they overcome. The word "church" is not mentioned after chapter three, and the vision moves from the things that are, to the things that will be in the future—primarily the Tribulation, the Antichrist, and the judgments leading to the return of Christ.

The dispensation of the age of grace began with Christ preaching and has continued to this present age. It is the fivefold ministry of the church (Eph. 4:11) that is responsible for advancing the message and power of the Kingdom of God to the inhabitants of the earth. In the book of Revelation there is a major transition in the vision from chapter three to chapter four. John transitions from the church to heaven in chapter four, then from heaven's viewpoint he witnesses the unleashing of numerous crises that strike the earth, initiated by four spirits riding four different colored spirit horses (Rev. 6:1-8). Some call the transition from the church to the Tribulation the "end of the church age."

The original purpose of the church was to bring together one unit of believers who would practice, preach, and promote the Kingdom of God on Earth. However, when the church began to divide over doctrinal interpretations, denominations were formed. Each denominational group allowed inside their "religious camp" only those people who were in full agreement with their biblical interpretations.

The church was supposed to preach the Gospel of the Kingdom (Matt. 24:14). They were supposed to demonstrate the power of the Kingdom, as revealed in the first message Christ preached in Nazareth: preach the Gospel to the poor, heal the brokenhearted, preach deliverance to the captives and recovery of sight to the blind, and set at liberty them that are bruised (Luke 4:16-18). The fullness of the Gospel is linked to the message of Christ reaching the known world, especially the Gentile nations.

THE SHAKING BEFORE THE INGATHERING

The spiritual principle of a shaking at the time of harvest is centered on the fact that every form of ancient harvest is separated and collected after some type of shaking.. There were seven different types of grains and fruits that grew in Israel:

- Barley

- Wheat

- Pomegranates

- Olives

- Figs

- Grapes

- Honey (dates)

Beginning with barley in early spring, each item harvested required some form of shaking. Barley must be winnowed by using a wooden winnowing fork to toss the grain in the air, and separate the stems and outer shell from the barley. The hard shell of wheat is separated by a threshing board that in Latin was called a "tribulim". When the stem and the chaff are removed from the heads of wheat, the chaff is burned in fire.

Olives on an olive tree can be handpicked; however, the ancient method was to use a long stick and hit the branches and loosen the olives. Grapes are separated from their vines by hand. To extract the juice, the grapes must be crushed using different methods. A pomegranate can be plucked from a tree and must be cut open to get the seeds or squeezed under pressure to obtain the juice.

Many parables of Christ indicate the need for a separation at the end of days, and specifically at the end-time harvest. For example:

- In the parable of the net, there is a separation of the good and bad fish

- In the parable of the wheat and tares, the tares are separated from the wheat

- In the parable of the sheep and goat, the goats are separated from the sheep

Harvest is a word used for the ingathering of some type of food, grains, and fruits. When the grain is in the field and the fruit is on the tree and still growing, it is not ready to be harvested. A ripening of the grains and fruits must occur first as an indicator that the time of the harvest has arrived. In Christ's parables, the harvest is the world (Greek: "age", see Matt. 13:39), meaning that at the time of the end, the hearts of men will be ripe, or open to the message of the Gospel.

Prior to the ingathering of the church to Christ in heaven, there will be a separation, which we clearly see now. It is growing wider, like a great gulf, and it is happening globally. In the United States, the nation is separated by ethnic group, religion, politics, moral values, and economic status. Christ warned that both wheat and tares will grow together in the same field at the same time, until the final harvest. The season of the good and bad seed populating the field of the world and the church is seen in our present age.

Within the contemporary church are doctrinal divisions that so oppose one another, a person would not believe the Bible was the source of some leaders' instructions. The Scripture warns against shedding innocent blood. Yet within the church are two opinions—one group says abortion is wrong, while the other sees nothing wrong with it, viewing it only as a medical procedure. God Himself spoke against men having sexual relations with men, and many Word-centered churches emphasize the covenant of marriage between a man and women. Others, however, proudly accept same sex relations as a lifestyle option, and even ordain people in same-sex relationships. These are examples of the wheat—children of the Kingdom—and the tares, who are children of darkness. Both lay claim to the same field, yet they must be separated at the end of the age.

Hebrews chapter 12 indicates there will be one more shaking of both the heavens and the earth. The heavenly shaking includes a collision in the cosmos in the second heaven, the powers of heaven being shaken, the stars from heaven falling to the earth, and destructive hurricanes and tornadoes. The shaking on the earth can refer to earthquakes and volcanic eruptions that will divide and devastate nations, continents, and people groups. Paul revealed the reason for the final shaking: "So that the things that cannot be shaken shall remain" (Heb. 12:27). Any shaking will remove things that need to be separated, but those true believers will be standing when the battle ends (Eph. 6:13).

MOVED BY FEAR TO PREPARE

Ministers who see the significance of biblical prophecy and passionately teach the subject must, in order to be true to the Scriptures, issue warnings to this generation, along with the blessed hope of Christ's return (Titus 2:13). Sadly, some members within the Body of Christ label these teachers as prophets of doom and gloom or negative soothsayers, often mocking and ostracizing them in certain church circles.

One of the main charges leveled against those who warn others are that ministers are promoting fear, and God has not given us the spirit of fear (2 Tim. 1:7).

Hebrews 11 is called the Bible's "heroes of faith" chapter. Noah, the builder of the ark, is one of numerous patriarchs listed in the hall of faith. Why was Noah inspired to build the ark? We read: "By faith Noah, being divinely warned of things not yet seen, moved with godly fear, prepared an ark for the saving of his household, by which he condemned the world and became heir of the righteousness which is according to faith" (Heb. 11:7).

Bible students are aware of Genesis 5:32 and 7:6, where Noah spent up to 100 years constructing a massive wooden ship to house his family and the animal population, which enabled both humans and animals to repopulate the earth following the global deluge. The phrase that stands out is: Noah was moved with godly fear to prepare an ark to save his house. The spirit of fear is completely opposite godly fear, or the fear of the Lord. A satanic spirit of fear is paralyzing, but the fear of the Lord is motivating. Let me explain.

I believe there is a literal heaven, the eternal abode of the righteous, and a literal hell, the final abode of the unrighteous. The thought of going to heaven is uplifting, encouraging, and motivating. But the thought of dying lost and spending eternity in hell is frightening. The godly fear of the Lord is a motivation for living according to Scripture, to avoid spending eternity separated from God and your righteous loved ones. Godly fear prevents a believer from living a careless, immoral, or carnal life, for fear of displeasing God and experiencing the chastisement or judgment that eventually comes to the disobedient.

The fear of the Lord is a positive motivation as we live our daily lives, because we know that one day we must all stand before Christ and give an account for our words and actions. At times, a person will refuse to serve Christ until days or hours before they know for certain their time has come to depart this life. The uncertainty of what lies beyond this life often strikes fear in the soon-to-be-eternal soul, and the heart responds to the unknown with a fear that leads to repentance.

The events that will surround the future Tribulation are so intense and dangerous that we read where men's hearts will fail them for fear, and for looking after those things which are coming on the earth (Luke 21:26). When those who hear warnings are void of Godly fear, they turn to mockery. Noah was mocked the entire time he prepared the ark and his immediate family—his wife, three sons, and their wives—were the only ones who entered the ark and survived the flood.

God will always send a sincere yet clear voice prior to major events of judgment. The Jewish historian Josephus was an eyewitness to Jerusalem's destruction in AD 70. In his writings, he recalled a man named Jesus who roamed the streets of the city for seven years and warned the inhabitants that their desolation was coming. In the seventh year, a rock from a Roman catapult struck him dead. His warning voice was silenced and the smoke of the temple darkened the sky.

MOVED BY GODLY DIRECTION, NOT HUMAN SPECULATION

A word of warning must be given here. Throughout seasons of Christian history, some have used prophetic signs and warnings to manipulate the masses and make outlandish predictions that never came to pass. People speculate by looking at a set of facts and guessing the outcome based on possibilities.

One of the great human needs is for security, which includes necessities such as shelter, water, clothing, and food. Food or water shortages can drive certain individuals to a mob mentality, where they are willing to harm others to obtain whatever they need or want. Years ago when the New Orleans levees broke, there was a fresh water shortage and no electricity. People broke through glass doors and pillaged stores as they grabbed anything and everything in sight. The threat of harm or danger can initiate more danger from those who themselves feel threatened.

I grew up hearing ministers preach on the return of Christ in a way that was so convicting and convincing, that I imagined at any moment the clouds would part like a scroll and the blast of a trumpet would shake the building. One of my earliest recollections was at age eleven, sitting in an open-air tabernacle in Roanoke, Virginia and listening to a powerful minister, Dr. T.L. Lowery, preach on the return of

Christ. I was sitting on a metal folding chair in the back of the tabernacle with some other young people, in awe of this man moving back and forth across the platform in his black suit and red tie, the sweat pouring down his face. What struck me was his statement, "Some of you young people think that when Jesus comes, you can grab hold of your father's coat tail and ride it up to the clouds. But if you are not ready to meet Christ, you will fall to the ground, left behind!" That was perhaps the first time I seriously prayed and asked the Lord to let me be ready for His return.

From my earliest years, I was always intrigued with the prophecies of the Bible, especially the return of the Lord. As I paid more attention to the Scriptures and preaching, I recalled a book by Hal Lindsey called *The Late Great Planet Earth* that revived interest in the prophetic Scriptures. I also became familiar with a term often used by evangelical Christians that identified the return of Christ for the church as "the rapture". I assumed at that time (this was the early 70s) that every Christian believed in this rapture event, and at least in my denominational circles, most did. However, once I began traveling as an evangelist in the 1980s, I soon learned that the rapture teaching was not only rejected by some, but was mocked and ridiculed by many ministers.

THE CHURCH AGE

Every dispensation of history, from Adam to the new covenant in Christ, had a specific moment of transition that ended one era and initiated another. Adam lived an unknown time in the Garden of Eden without knowledge of sin, meaning he dwelt in a time of human innocence. After eating from the tree of the knowledge of good and evil, the human conscience became aware of sin and the sin nature. Innocence died and guilt was birthed.

After Adam, a generation of righteous men sought God, yet there was no written moral code or judicial instruction on Earth until the giving of the Law on Mount Sinai (see Ex. 20). The dispensation of the Law continued for about 1,500 years until the public ministry of John the Baptist, who was the forerunner to the Messiah. The new dispensation that would be released to the world was the Kingdom dispensation, which would spread throughout the earth the message of a new covenant. Luke explained: "For the law and prophets were until John: since that time the kingdom of God is preached, and every man presseth into it" (Luke 16:16).

This Kingdom has laws (the Bible), ambassadors (ministers of the Gospel), a King (Jesus Christ), and even their own language (new tongues). Presently the Kingdom is visible through the body of Christ operating under Christ's delegated authority. When the dispensation of the church age concludes, the King Himself with His armies of heaven will return to Earth and set up His throne in Jerusalem. I believe the point that moves the world from God's grace to His wrath is the transitioning of the believers from Earth to heaven through the catching away and the resurrection of the dead in Christ.

The sooner the church completes its assignment to preach the Gospel to all nations of the world, the sooner the end will come.

CHAPTER 12

ARGUMENTS AGAINST THE PRE-TRIBULATION GATHERING

I HAVE EMPHASIZED THE significance of God's divine order that is evident throughout the Scriptures. In the tabernacle and later the temple, there was the Outer Court, the Inner Count, and the Holy of Holies. The Israelites could enter the Outer Court, but never pass beyond a certain border that guarded the other two chambers. Levites had access to both the Outer and Inner Courts. However, no Levite could access the sacred Holy of Holies without coming under an immediate death sentence. The high priest alone passed beyond the temple veil into the Holy of Holies once a year on the Day of Atonement. It is impossible to reverse the order of approach by making the Holy of Holies the entrance point.

If we theologically switch the order of the festivals, we change God's set pattern and design for future prophetic events to fit our own agenda or theories. Despite this fact, there are people whose arguments counter this pattern. For example, some point out that, in Scripture, the word *trumpets* (including the festival) can refer to more types of trumpets than just a picture of the rapture.

Without any doubt, the next festival to follow Pentecost (the church age) is the Feast of Trumpets. The emphasis on this day is the blowing of numerous trumpets. In the book of Revelation, a series of trumpet judgments occur during the first forty-two months of the seven-year

Tribulation. Some people believe that the Feast of Trumpets and the rapture will occur at the sound of the seventh angel blasting the seventh trumpet.

Unless a person has in-depth knowledge of the Scriptures, Hebrew customs, and Hebrew understanding of patterns, this theory seems correct at face value. It is commonly taught and accepted by many Christians in the western world. As a result, when I teach a pre-Tribulation rapture, I am inundated with mail calling me everything from a deceiver to a heretic.

Most prophetic teachers acknowledge that the Tribulation begins with the signing of a seven-year treaty (Dan. 9:27). In the midst of this seven years, the Antichrist will break this agreement, invade Egypt, Libya, and Ethiopia, and bring the people of those nations under his rule (see Dan. 11:42-43). After this is where the theories divide.

Those who believe in a pre-Tribulation gathering mark the rapture either before, during, or shortly after the signing of the seven-year treaty. Some believe the rapture could occur before, during, or after the war of Ezekiel 38 and 39, called the war of Gog and Magog. One reason for adding the Ezekiel war scenario is because the prophet mentioned it will take seven years to destroy (burn) the weapons from this war (Ezek. 39:9). This appears to align with the seven-year agreement of Daniel 9:27. If this is correct, then the pre-Tribulation coming of Christ is linked with the timing of this war.

In the order of John's vision, when Christ breaks the seventh seal on the mysterious seven-sealed book (see Revelation 5-9), then seven angels step forward, prepared with seven trumpets to sound. Six specific judgments are unleashed on Earth as the trumpets are sounded:

- The first angel releases hail and fire that burns a third of trees and all green grass (8:7)

- The second angel releases a burning mountain, which destroys a third of the sea life and ships (8:8-9)

- The third angel releases an asteroid that destroys a third of the rivers and waters (8:10-11)

- The fourth angel causes the sun, moon and stars to be darkened on a third of the earth (8:12)

- The fifth angel releases strange creatures from the abyss that will torment men (9:1-11)

- The sixth angel releases fallen angels currently bound under the Euphrates River who will kill a third of men (9:14-15)

The seventh angel, however, is an angel of transition. When John saw this angel he was instructed to "eat a small book," and told that he would prophecy to many nations (Rev. 10:11). Another amazing word came to John at the time he saw the seventh angel, who was sounding a trumpet and announcing the soon completion of the "mystery of God."

> "But in the days of the sounding of the seventh angel, when he is about to sound, the mystery of God would be finished, as he declared to his servants the prophets."
>
> – REVELATION 10:7 (NKJV)

Mid-Tribulation believers use the following points as they attempt to place the rapture at this timeframe. First, this is the last angel in the book of Revelation to sound a trumpet. The reasoning is, since this is the last trumpet blasted from heaven, this must be the "last trump" Paul mentioned in 1 Corinthians 15:52 when he said we will be changed: "...in a moment, in the twinkling of an eye, at the last trumpet. For the trumpet will sound, and the dead will be raised incorruptible, and we shall be changed."

Their second point is the significance of the phrase "the mystery of God." Mid-Tribulation teachers apply this back to Paul's statement in 1 Corinthians 15 where he wrote that believers will experience a change from mortality to immortality, and wrote: "Behold I show you a mystery: we shall not all sleep, but we shall all be changed" (1 Cor. 15:51). Since the seventh angel uses the word *mystery*, the mid-Tribulation teachers say that this "mystery" refers back to Paul's mystery of the gathering together and the resurrection of the dead in Christ. Thus, the belief is that the "mystery of God" mentioned in Revelation is the same mystery that Paul referred to in 1 Corinthians 15:51.

A third point is the flow of events in Revelation. Moving forward from Revelation 10:7 to Revelation 11:18, John witnessed the Judgment Seat of Christ in heaven, where all saints are judged to receive rewards. Notice this judgment followed the announcement of the mystery of God being finished:

> "And the nations were angry, and thy wrath is come, and the time of the dead, that they should be judged, and that thou shouldest give reward unto thy servants the prophets, and to the saints, and them that fear thy name, small and great; and shouldest destroy them which destroy the earth."
>
> – REVELATION 11:18 (KJV)

Two judgments are set to occur—the judgment seat of Christ referred to here, and the great white throne judgment mentioned in Revelation 20:11-15, which takes place at the conclusion of Christ's one-thousand-year reign on Earth. For the judgment seat of Christ to be recorded in Revelation 11, all believers from the New Covenant era must be in heaven, as Paul wrote, "We must all appear before the judgment seat of Christ..." (2 Cor. 5:10). Revelation 11 to 13 is the mid-point of the seven-year Tribulation. This judgment does occur in heaven at the same time the earth is transitioning to the slaying of the two witnesses and the Antichrist invading Jerusalem. Since believers are in heaven following the seventh angel's announcement, the assumption is that the seventh trumpet was the "trump of God," and the church goes through the first half of the Tribulation.

The question becomes, when do the believers arrive in heaven? Is it at that moment, or long before that moment? The answer to this enigma is found in understanding the significance of the "last trump."

THE LAST TRUMP

Is the final trumpet sounded by the seventh angel the "last trump" that Paul referred to in 1 Corinthians 15:52? There are difficulties with this theory. First, let's consider the timeframe of Paul's words and John's vision. Scholars date Paul's letter to the church at Corinth around AD 54. In his epistle, the imagery of a last trump was *not a mystery* to any Jew within the church. The Jews understood the blowing of shofars and silver trumpets during their new moons, Sabbaths, and yearly festivals (see Numbers 10; Psalms 81:3). The Jews were also keenly aware of the Festival of Trumpets, when over one hundred trumpet blasts are sounded. Paul, being a devout Jew who understood the Torah and Jewish tradition, knew that on the Feast of Trumpets, several different types of blasts were noted by their length—both long and short blasts.

The Feast of Trumpets, also known as Rosh Hashanah, is the Jewish secular New Year. It is also called Yom Teruah in Hebrew, and is set to occur on the Jewish calendar on the first day of the seventh month of Tishrei. The Jewish tradition is that on this day the earth was created by God, marking the festival as the beginning of the six days of creation and the creation of Adam and Eve.

During a typical Rosh Hashanah service, the shofar (ram's horn) is blown one hundred times to fulfill the commandment to make a teruah (a noise on the shofar). Rabbinical sources teach that four different sounds from the shofar are heard on this day. They are represented by the following Hebrew words:

1. Tekia—a long single blast (representing the sound of the King's coronation)

2. Sshevarim—three short wail-like blasts (signifying brokenness and repentance)

3. Teruah—nine staccato blasts of alarm (to awaken the soul)

4. Tekiah Hagadol—a great and long final blast

If we compare these blasts to the New Testament Scriptures about the resurrection and gathering together, we find parallels. The "trump of God" (1 Thess. 4:16) is not just the announcement that the Lord has returned. In Revelation, Jesus the High Priest will become the King of Kings in preparation to rule on Earth (Rev. 19:16). The tekia is the invitation to the King's coronation in heaven.

The second sound (shevarim) signifies the brokenness of those who will be left behind, knowing what lies ahead, and their sorrow for missing Christ's return. In the parable of the goodman and his house, when the thief came, his house was divided and he was sorrowful (Matt. 24:43).

The third sound, the teruah, is the awakening of the dead in Christ, as this is identified as the sound that awakens the soul. Those who are alive at the return of Christ will be changed at the sound of the last trump. Here is where the fourth blast is linked to Paul's statement.

The fourth shofar sound is the tekiah hagadol, known as the longest and loudest sound of all other trumpets. It is the final trumpet blast that concludes the Feast of Trumpets. This is the same loud and long sound that Moses heard on Mount Sinai prior to God coming down and him going up to meet the Lord:

> "And when the blast of the trumpet sounded long and became louder and louder, Moses spoke, and God answered him by voice. Then the LORD came down upon Mount Sinai, on the top of the mountain. And the LORD called Moses to the top of the mountain, and Moses went up."
>
> – EXODUS 19:19-20 (NKJV)

The loud and long blast, the tekiah hagadol, was the sound calling Moses up to meet the Lord on the mount, just as at the last trump, those believers who are alive will be "caught up to meet the Lord in the air." (1 Thess. 4:17). The pattern for the rapture is evident in Exodus 19.

The Exodus Narrative	The New Testament Rapture Narrative
The Lord came down in a cloud (19:9)	Christ will return in clouds (1 Thess. 4:17)
The people were to be ready on the third day (19:11)	We are raised on the third day (Hosea 6:2)

There was thunder and lightning (19:16)	Christ will return as lightning (Matt. 24:27)
There was a loud voice of a trumpet (19:16)	The trump will sound (1 Cor. 15:52)
The Lord descended (19:18)	The Lord himself shall descend (1 Thess. 4:16)
The trumpet sounded louder and long (19:19)	The loud and long trumpet is the "last trump"
The voice of God was heard (19:19)	The voice of the archangel (1 Thess. 4:16)
Moses went up (19:20)	The living will be caught up (1 Thess. 4:17)

From the Hebraic perspective and from Scripture, there is ample evidence to indicate that the "last trump" that sounds to catch up the living has nothing whatsoever to do with the seventh angel. If Paul's audience at Corinth had not understood what he meant by the "last trump," he would have written more commentary in response to their questions about it. When Paul wrote 1 Thessalonians, he followed up with a second epistle to clarify in detail his revelation on the rapture and return of Christ. Paul's second letter to the Corinthians has no follow up on the rapture, resurrection or last trump, as the Jews understood that the last trump is linked to the Festival of Trumpets.

Another point is that when Paul revealed the catching up and resurrection in 1 Thessalonians 4:16, he said there would be *three elements all at once*, not just a trumpet blast. He wrote that we would hear a shout, followed by the voice of the archangel, followed by the trump of God. To make these three elements fit the seventh angel scenario, some note in Revelation 10:4 where "seven thunders uttered their voices," and John was told to seal up the utterings and not to write them. Mid-Tribulation followers use this narrative to mark these voices as the shout Paul referred to in 1 Thessalonians 4:16. This is stretching a verse to accommodate a theory and has no reference to the shout we will hear when Christ returns.

The Greek word Paul used for "shout" in 1 Thessalonians 4:16 is not plural (many shouts), but singular (one shout). The word is *keleusma* and means, *a call, a summons; a shout or command.* This shout is the singular voice of the Lord commanding the dead to rise. Christ said in John 5:28 to "marvel not at this: for the hour is coming, in which all that are in the graves shall hear his voice, and come forth." In John 5:25 Christ said "...the dead shall hear the voice of the Son of God; and they that hear shall live." Since the dead in Christ rise first, this shout would be a command for them to come forth. Since Christ alone is the resurrection and the life, this shout must come directly from Him, from the clouds, when all righteous souls in the grave will hear Him!

The angel in Revelation 10 that comes down with a cloud and a rainbow is not Christ coming to raise the dead or catch away the living in the middle of the Tribulation. There is no indication whatsoever of this in the text. This mighty angel is standing on Earth, with one foot on the land and one in the sea. his hand upraised to heaven (Rev. 10:1-7), which is the same imagery seen in Daniel 12:7. In Daniel, the angel is declaring that the last half of the Tribulation is set for "a time, times, and a half" (forty-two months) and the power of the holy people will be scattered.

In Revelation, this angel is not collecting saints and bringing them to heaven, but is presenting a book (scroll) for John to eat. I believe John was given the book of Daniel, whose symbolism and understanding would be "sealed until the time of the end" (see Dan. 12:9). Since John was seeing the time of the end in a vision, God unlocked Daniel's visions that were concealed, revealing many new details to John. Daniel's vision was sealed, but John was told not to seal his vision (Rev. 22:10).

Evidence of the Daniel—John connection is observed three chapters later in Revelation chapter 13, where John saw the same beast that Daniel saw in three different forms (see Daniel 7). However, John saw all three beast kingdoms (Babylon, Media-Persia, and Greece) coming together to form one final, dangerous empire. From the moment this angel gave John the mysterious book and he ate the scroll, and the seventh angel sounded, John began to see the future beast kingdom, its seven heads, and its ten horns—all imagery found in Daniel (see

Revelation 13). John also saw a false prophet rising from the earth, an image Daniel never saw (Rev. 13:11-18).

The mystery the angel spoke of in Revelation 10 was not the mystery of the resurrection and physical change to immortality at Christ's return. It was not the same mystery of which Paul spoke. Paul was an apostle (not a prophet), and Revelation 10:7 says that when the angel sounds his trumpet, the "mystery of God should be finished, as he hath declared to his servants the prophets." What mystery did the prophets speak of? The Old Testament prophets were men from the time of Enoch to Malachi, with Malachi (according to *Jewish* belief) being the final prophet to pen sacred Scripture. This mystery of God that the angel unlocked to John was the mystery of the "time, times, and dividing of time" that Daniel spoke of. It was an announcement to finish God's plan which climaxes at the conclusion of the second part of the Tribulation, and not Paul's resurrection mystery.

After eating the scroll, John penned the next vision, which begins in chapter 11 with two witnesses and their deaths. The apocalyptic events that begin following the seventh angel's announcement are unlocked and understood by John, but they were first seen hundreds of years earlier by the prophets Daniel and Zechariah.

When Paul spoke of the mystery in 1 Corinthians, he was not emphasizing the mystery of a trumpet blast, but answering the question about how God would raise someone from the dead when their bodies have gone back to the earth.

> "But someone will say, "How are the dead raised up? And with what body do they come?" Foolish one, what you sow is not made alive unless it dies. And what you sow, you do not sow that body that shall be, but mere grain—perhaps wheat or some other grain. But God gives it a body as He pleases, and to each seed its own body."
>
> – 1 CORINTHIANS 15:35-38

Paul then comments:

> "So also is the resurrection of the dead. The body is sown in corruption, it is raised in incorruption. It is sown in dishonor, it is raised in glory. It is sown in weakness, it is raised in power. It is

sown a natural body, it is raised a spiritual body. There is a natural body, and there is a spiritual body."

— 1 CORINTHIANS 15:42-44

Paul referred to this process of a seed dying then coming to life again as the same process when a believer dies, returns to the dust (Gen. 3:19), and is raised to life again. Paul then proceeds to explain this mystery by revealing how those living will be changed in a moment, in the twinkling of an eye at the sound of the last trump.

THE VOICE OF A TRUMP

In apocalyptic and at times other biblical imagery, trumpets are described as having a *voice*. John spoke of the "other voices of the trumpet of three angels" (Rev. 8:13). Could the "trump of God" actually be a manifestation of the audible voice of God? Paul never explains what this "trump of God" actually is, whether it is a literal trumpet or a metaphor for God's voice. In the Torah, when Moses was on Mount Sinai and God spoke, His voice is described as a *trumpet*. Notice in Exodus 19:19, when God comes down on Mount Sinai and Moses goes up, there is a "voice of a trumpet sounding loud and long." This same thought is expressed by John after his messages to the seven churches. After the last church is addressed, John said, "I heard behind me the voice of a trumpet saying coming up here..." (Rev. 4:1). In Exodus 19, when the trumpet waxed long and loud, we then read, "God answered him by voice" (Exod. 19:19). Immediately after God's voice is heard, the next verse reads, "And the Lord came down upon Mount Sinai, on the top of the mount; and the Lord called Moses to the top of the mount; and Moses went up" (Exod. 19:20).

Another important point is that Paul's trump of God is a singular trump; not many trumpets, but one in particular. This is not the trumpet of the seventh angel. Paul's trump is the final trumpet blast, the loudest and longest sound blown on the Festival of Trumpets. The patterns of the rapture are concealed in the Exodus 19 narrative, when Moses met God face-to-face on the top of Mount Sinai. Exodus 19 is parallel to Paul's rapture revelation found in 1 Thessalonians 4:16-17: "The Lord Himself shall descend...and we who are alive shall be caught up together with them in the clouds to meet the Lord in the air...".

THE POST-TRIBULATION TRUMPET

Several of my friends are convinced that the post-Tribulation view is the most biblical, meaning Christ will return on the last day of the seven-year Tribulation. Again, the trumpet is used to undergird this theory. Some post-Tribulation believers place the announcement of the seventh angel at end of the seven-year Tribulation, which in both the setting and context of John's vision is impossible. The seventh angel marks the mid-point of the Tribulation and not the conclusion. To make the theory fit, they match the seven trumpet judgments with the seven vial judgments in Revelation 16:1-21, and teach that these are the same judgments released by the angel's trumpet judgments. From chapters 6 through 17 are two series of judgments: one occurs during the first half of the Tribulation and another during the second half when the angels pour out the bowls. The bowls (called vials in the KJV) include several different judgments not listed among the seven trumpet judgments, such as the sun scorching men with great heat (16:9); sores on men who have the mark of the beast (16:11); the drying up of the Euphrates River (16:12); and the collapse and destruction of Mystery Babylon (Rev. 17), all which occur during the last forty-two months of the Tribulation.

The main verses used to assert a post-Tribulation return of Christ for the church are found in the Olivet Discourse in Matthew 24. After Christ warned of a cosmic shaking of the heavens we read:

> "Immediately after the tribulation of those days the sun will be darkened, and the moon will not give its light; the stars will fall from heaven, and the powers of the heavens will be shaken. Then the sign of the Son of Man will appear in heaven, and then all of the tribes of the earth will mourn, and they will see the Son of Man coming on the clouds of heaven with power and great glory. And He will send His angels with a great sound of a trumpet, and they will gather together His elect from the four winds, from one end of heaven to the other."
>
> – MATTHEW 24:29-31 (NKJV)

First, they point to the sun, moon and stars being darkened, which coincides with the sixth seal of Revelation 6. They note that when Christ returns at the end of the Tribulation, He will send angels with the sound of a trumpet to gather His elect from the four regions of the earth. The post-Tribulation teachers identify the "elect" as the church, thus saying this verse teaches that Christ will sound the trumpet to gather Christians from around the world to Him in Jerusalem. The fact that angels sound a trumpet enforces in their minds that this is the moment of the return.

This prediction of angels collecting the elect is first penned by Isaiah. This major prophet wrote:

> "And it shall come to pass in that day, that the great trumpet shall be blown, and they shall come which were ready to perish in the land of Assyria, and the outcasts in the land of Egypt, and they shall worship the Lord in the holy mount at Jerusalem."
>
> – ISAIAH 27:13 (KJV)

Isaiah used the words *great trumpet*, and Christ repeated this when He said, *a great sound of a trumpet*. Those *ready to perish* are those surviving the Tribulation as they were *outcasts*. The Hebrew word is *dachah*, from a root that means *to push down*. Christ in His discourse called these His *elect*, referring to the Jews near death.

Another Scripture reference often used by post-Tribulation teachers is that of the separation of the wheat and the tares. Wheat represents the children of the Kingdom of God, and the tares represent the children of Satan. Both grow together until harvest time. We read:

> "The enemy who sowed them is the devil, the harvest is the end of the age, and the reapers are the angels. Therefore as the tares are gathered and burned in the fire, so it will be at the end of this age. The Son of Man will send out His angels, and they will gather out of His kingdom all things that offend, and those who practice lawlessness, and will cast them into the furnace of fire. There will be wailing and gnashing of teeth."
>
> – MATTHEW 13:39-42 (NKJV)

First, consider the angels gathering *the elect* in Matthew 24:31. I debated a minister on television who said the *elect* that Christ was speaking of is the church, and the church is going through all of the Tribulation to be gathered "after the tribulation" (Matt. 24:29). I reminded him that the word *elect* is used in various contexts, not just concerning individuals within the church. For example:

- The Messiah is the elect (Isa 42:1)

- Israel is called God's elect (Isa. 45:4; 65:22)

- Judah is called the elect (Isa. 65:9)

- Angels of God are called the elect (1 Tim. 5:21)

- Christ is called the elect (1 Pet. 2:6)

- A distinguished woman in the church was called the elect lady (2 John 1)

- Another woman in the church was called your elect sister (2 John 13)

Eklektos, the Greek word for "elect", refers to one who is favored above another. In the 1611 KJV it is translated as chosen and elect. In Matthew 24, the reference to elect is not connected in any manner or form with the church. Christ's discourse was given prior to the birth of the church on Pentecost (Acts 2:1-4). Christ's discourse in Matthew 24 was to an entirely Jewish audience, to people raised in or around synagogues, who were familiar with the Torah and the predictions of the biblical prophets. When Christ spoke of the Tribulation, Jewish believers could have recalled Daniel's prediction of a "time of trouble" for Israel in which God would deliver those whose names are written in the heavenly book (Dan. 12:1). God made it clear to Daniel that the *seventy weeks prophecy* was for Israel. The angel Gabriel (Dan. 9:21) informed Daniel:

"Seventy weeks are determined upon thy people and upon the holy city; to finish the transgression, and to make an end of sins...and to anoint the most holy."

– Daniel 9:24 (KJV)

Seventy weeks (or 490 years) concludes, according to Daniel 9:27 with one final *week*, which in Hebrew is seven years. This last seven years begins when the Antichrist confirms the covenant with many for one week (Dan. 9:27). This last seven years is set aside for Israel, the Jews, and Jerusalem. This seven-year period of time, which will lead them to the knowledge of the Messiah, has no direct bearing on the true church in the body of Christ. The overcoming believers who pray, fast, and use their spiritual authority are, presently the primary barrier that helps restrain evil. Paul taught that the restrainer must be taken out of the way, and then the man of sin (the Antichrist) can be revealed in his full identity (see 2 Thessalonians 2:7-8).

I often hear ministers tell believers that the Tribulation is for the church and that all living believers endure it by barely surviving, or at some point dying by beheading. One question that arises with this theory is, why would God allow the supernatural sealing of 144,000 Jews in order to protect them from the Antichrist, his armies, and the judgments striking the earth (see Revelation 7), yet Christ's bride be required to face the Antichrist without the same type of protection? Not one of the 144,000 Jewish men will be harmed or martyred in the Tribulation, yet we are to believe that Christ will remove protection from millions of His own covenant believers? It was Christ who said that we should pray to "be found worthy to escape these things" (Luke 21:36) and Paul who taught that "God has not appointed us to wrath" (1 Thess. 5:9). Why pray to be worthy to escape if the church is marked to go through all of the Tribulation? What type of escape is this?

Another often overlooked point is the church's earthly assignment. We are to go into all the world and preach the Gospel to every creature (Mark 16:15). The global spread of the Gospel is a prophetic key that introduces both the time of the end and the Tribulation. Christ taught that the "Gospel of the kingdom shall be preached in all the world as a witness to all nations, and then the end shall come" (Matt. 24:14). Under the dispensation of the grace of God, the responsibility of preaching the Gospel is solely in the hands of the church. That assignment cannot be altered, changed, or transferred as long as the church is thriving and active on this planet.

This brings up another interesting point. During the first half of the seven-year Tribulation, two prophets (who many believe will be Elijah and Enoch) will suddenly appear in Jerusalem and proclaim a specific message. They will demonstrate acts of judgment, such as withholding rain for forty-two months, turning water to blood, and striking the earth with plagues. If anyone tries to harm them, fire will proceed from their mouths and devour their enemies (Rev. 11:5-6). These two men will be such a central focus that, after forty-two months when they are slain by the Antichrist, the world rejoices and even sends gifts to one another (Rev. 11:10) to celebrate the death of these prophets who tormented them (Rev. 11:10).

During the first part of the Tribulation, 144,000 Jewish men are set apart by the Lord and protected from the violent beast and his kingdom (Rev. 7:1-8). These men are on Earth the same time as the two prophets (Rev. 11:1-10). If the church is still on Earth the first forty-two months, then why is the church not continuing to preach? The answer is that the church will continue to preach until the conclusion of the dispensation of the grace of God, which concludes the very day of the rapture.

Following the rapture, when the first forty-two months of the Tribulation begin, the two witnesses enter the scene and preach the Gospel—the message of the Messiah. Then they are slain. Once they are slain, the Antichrist will seize Jerusalem and the false prophet will make an icon ("image" in the KJV) and cause it to speak and live. Those who do not worship the image will be killed (Rev. 13:11-16). This order in Revelation is important to understanding the prophetic order of events. Christ said:

> "And this gospel of the kingdom will be preached in all the
> world as a witness unto all nations, and then the end will come.
> Therefore when you shall see the abomination of desolation,

spoken of by Daniel the prophet, standing in a holy place (who-
soever reads, let him understand), then let those who are in Judea
flee to the mountains."

– MATTHEW 24:14-15 (NKJV)

This abomination that Matthew confessed he did not understand
was later revealed to John in Revelation. In the Old Testament, idolatry was always considered an abomination; and in the Tribulation,
when the false prophet speaks life to a man-made idol, causing it to
speak and live, this is the abomination. This satanic miracle will "make
Jerusalem desolate." Mid-Tribulation proponents say: the Gospel is
preached by the church, and then the abomination happens. They
theorize that since this happens in the middle of the Tribulation
(Revelation 11), then the church will be on Earth preaching for the
first half of the Tribulation.

This sounds like a valid interpretation, until we understand that
once the church is removed at the beginning of the Tribulation, the
Gospel is still preached through the two witnesses. Once they are
slain in the middle of the Tribulation, then the abomination is set up.
This happens in the exact order Christ gave in Matthew 24:14-15.

Many mid- and post-Tribulation followers emphasize that it is necessary for the church to go through the Tribulation for the purpose of
persecution and purging. This makes little sense, since the purging of
the body, soul and spirit does not occur through some form of persecution. It is accomplished through the finished work of Christ. This
theory is works-centered, meaning that purification comes through
my actions during extreme persecution, or the shedding of my own
blood by beheading. Some suggest it is unfair for this generation not
to endure deadly persecution, since believers for centuries have had
to endure serious opposition for the Gospel. However, consider that
believers from around the world are now being persecuted, especially
in Islamic nations, India, parts of Africa, and other places. Under ISIS
in Iraq and Syria, thousands of Christians, including children, have
been tortured, beheaded, and crucified for not denying Christ. This
absolutely is a tribulation and time of distress for those in the middle
of the crisis, but it is not *the Great* Tribulation. The Great Tribulation

is not just Satan becoming angry; it is also the *wrath of God* and the *wrath of the Lamb* (Rev. 6:16; 14:19; 19:15).

THE CONFUSION OF ISRAEL AND THE CHURCH

Much of the confusion in the mid- and post-Tribulation schools of thought could be cleared up with one important change in their interpretation: Do not mix Scriptures that are specifically written for Israel and the Jews with verses that apply to the church and believers. In Daniel's future predictions, for example, his dreams, visions, and angelic instructions point to the final ten kings, the beast kingdom, and the future Tribulation. He was informed that, during that time, the adversary will "wear out the saints of the Most High" (Dan. 7:25). When the time of trouble concludes, the saints will "take the kingdom" (Dan. 7:18) and "judgment (over the kingdom) will be given to the saints" (Dan. 7:22).

Some prophetic teachers connect the saints in Daniel's future visions with the church, using Daniel 7:25 as proof that the church will be on Earth during the Tribulation and God will allow the Antichrist to "wear out the saints," or the church. However, the entire seventy weeks prophecy, including the final week of seven years (Dan. 9:24, 12:1), is a set period of prophetic sabbaticals designed for Israel, the Jews, and Jerusalem. The portions of the book of Daniel that point to the Gentiles are the animal symbolism and the dream of the metallic image, which reveal the Gentile empires ruling from the time of Babylon to the time of the end. All of these have in the past or will in the future impact Israel in some manner (see Daniel chapters 2, 7 and 8).

The word *saints* is found seven times in six verses in Daniel, all in chapter seven (7:18, 21, 22 [twice], 25 and 27. This portion of Daniel was written in Aramaic and the word saints is *qaddiysh*, which corresponds to the Hebrew word *qadosh*, meaning "a holy one". Three things are called holy: angels (Matt. 25:31), saints of God (1 Peter 1:15, 1 Cor. 1:2), and the sanctuary where God is worshipped (Heb. 9:24-25). The word "saints" is found thirty-five times in thirty-six verses in the Old Testament and is used to identify people who are in covenant with God, and who walk in truth and righteousness. There will be a righteous Jewish remnant on Earth during the first part of the Tribulation, and they will be identified by the Father's name in their foreheads (Rev 7:1-8).

In the Old Testament, it is righteous Jews who are called saints. The New Testament church was non-existent in Daniel's time, and no prophecy in Daniel can specifically be applied to the church, although the verses related to the Messiah's return to Earth include all saints (holy ones), both Jew and Gentile.

One post-Tribulation theory said that all Christians will remain on Earth until Christ returns on the last day of the Tribulation with the "armies of heaven" (see Revelation 19:14, 19) to set up His rule in Jerusalem. The theory is that all Christians living at that moment will be changed suddenly when the angels sound the trumpet for the elect (Matt. 24:31), and all living believers are given an immortal body. Suddenly they will be "caught up to meet Christ in the clouds," (1 Thess. 4:17), then immediately return back to Earth. I call this the "U-turn return," as believers go up, do a U-turn, then come back down. This theory points out that John saw the armies in heaven on white horses, and this army is a host of heavenly angels and not the church or believers coming from heaven with Christ.

This theory is contrary to the vision of Zechariah, who saw the Messiah ascending from heaven to the Mount of Olives. We read:

> "And his feet shall stand in that day upon the Mount of Olives, which is before Jerusalem on the east, and the Mount of Olives shall cleave in the midst thereof toward the east and toward the west...and the Lord my God shall come and all the saints with thee."
>
> – ZECHARIAH 14:4-5 (KJV)

In this reference, the saints that Zechariah saw would be the family of God, including Abraham, Isaac, Jacob (Matt. 8:11), and all first covenant and new covenant believers, who return from heaven to rule with Christ for one thousand years. There are two distinct returns of the Messiah found in the New Testament:

The Rapture Return	The Reigning Return
The day and hour is unknown (Matt. 25:13)	The day is the last day of the Tribulation
Only believers see this return (Heb. 9:28)	Every eye shall see him (Rev. 1:7)
This return is for the believers (1 John 3:2-3)	This return is with the believers (Rev. 19:14)
This return takes believers to heaven (John 14:1-4)	This return brings believers from heaven (Rev. 19:14)
This return releases the Great Tribulation	This return concludes the Great Tribulation
This return releases Satan's wrath (Rev. 12:12)	This return brings an end to Satan (Rev. 20:1-3)

The true believers are not on Earth during the seven years of the Great Tribulation. The book of Revelation is divided in two halves: forty-two months and forty-two months, or 1,260 days and 1,260 days (Rev. 11:2; 12:6; 13:5). At the beginning of the Tribulation, John described a worship scene with the living creatures and elders, and the elders sing a song to the Lamb and proclaim, "...for thou wast slain, and has redeemed us to God by thy blood out of every kindred, and tongue, and people, and nation" (Rev. 5:9). Then in chapter seven is a multitude from every nation waving palm branches and blessing God. These came out of the Great Tribulation and "have washed their robes, and made them white in the blood of the Lamb" (Rev. 7:12-14). In Revelation is an important observation regarding the saints in heaven:

> "The nations were angry, and Your wrath has come, and the time of the dead, that they should be judged, and that You should reward Your servants the prophets and the saints, and those who fear Your name, small and great, and should destroy those who destroy the earth."
>
> – Rev. 11:18 (NKJV)

In Revelation chapter 6, Christ begins the Tribulation process with the breaking of the first seal on the seven sealed scroll (Rev. 6:1-2). A group of redeemed are worshipping in heaven prior to the revelation of this scroll. In Revelation chapter 7, a great multitude has made their robes white and come out of the Great Tribulation (Rev. 7:14). People debate the phrase "made their robes white." Dr. Ray Brubaker, founder of *God's News Behind the News,* studied Greek at Moody Bible Institute and noted that the Greek word indicates that these were individuals whose robes were tarnished. Therefore, they were not part of the original raptured group, but went through a brief portion of the Tribulation and *made* their robes white by the blood of Christ.

Whatever the case, in Revelation 11:18, those who were caught up, as well as those who had been dead and were raised, are called to this judgment where they will be rewarded for their faithfulness. Those being judged are "prophets, saints, and those who fear God's name" (Rev. 11:18). After the death of the two witnesses, the world enters the halfway point of the seven-year Tribulation. In John's vision, believers are already in heaven receiving rewards, which means that based upon the chronological flow of the book of Revelation, the church is in heaven long before the conclusion of the Tribulation.

When Jesus ate and drank with His disciples prior to His crucifixion, He said that He would not eat and drink the supper again until He ate and drank it anew in His Father's kingdom (Matt. 26:29). This will be fulfilled when the saints are called to the marriage supper of the Lamb (Rev. 19:7-9). John revealed that the wife of the Lamb has made herself ready and is clothed in fine linen, clean and white.

Some suggest that the New Jerusalem, rather than the church, is the bride of Christ. However, a city made with gemstones cannot sit at a table and eat a meal. A city is not clothed in white linen, which is the "righteousness of the saints" (Rev. 19:8). The bride of Christ is, unquestionably, the church. Based upon the New Testament Scriptures, while on Earth the church is the "body of Christ" (see Rom. 7:4; 1 Cor. 10:16-17; 12:13-27). Once the church, which is made up of believers from all nations, is taken to heaven, we are presented at the marriage supper as the "bride of Christ." Paul instructed the church, being engaged to Christ, to be faithful and pure:

> "For I am jealous over you with a godly jealousy. For I have betrothed you to one husband that I may present you as a chaste virgin to Christ."
>
> – 2 CORINTHIANS 11:2 (NKJV)

The heavenly wedding supper is the consummation for the groom (Christ) and the bride (the church). It occurs during the last year of the seven-year Tribulation. In the Torah, when a man and woman married they were given one year off from manual labor (see Deut. 24:5). Perhaps this same pattern is repeated when the bride and groom unite at the great supper. As the harlot religious system is destroyed on Earth during the final year of the Tribulation, the bride will be in heaven, preparing to return with the King to retake an Earth that has been controlled by Satan for thousands of years.

THOUGHTS FROM THE EARLY FATHERS

Post-Tribulation followers often point out that some of the early church fathers, men such as Irenaeus, Hippolytus and others, taught that the Antichrist would arise and persecute the church. Because some of these early fathers were born shortly after the Apocalypse was written, some suggest that John himself must have believed this post-Tribulation view. Some teach that these men's beliefs are absolute proof of a post-Tribulation return of the Messiah. I like to point out that, while most of the fathers taught solid biblical doctrine, they disagreed about the interpretation of certain doctrines.

Several church fathers and writers taught that the Roman Emperor Nero would eventually return from hell and become the dreaded Antichrist. These writings included the Sibylline Oracles, a commentary of Jewish and Christian prophecies penned in the first or second century AD; a Christian poet named Commodian; and a fourth century writer named Sulpicius Severus who, after recounting Nero's wicked rule, taught that many believed he (Nero) would come before the Antichrist. As late as the fifth century, Augustine commented on

Paul's statement in 2 Thessalonians 2:7 and said that "the mystery of iniquity is already working." He was referring to Emperor Nero, who ruled at the time of Paul's writing, and that some supposed would rise again and be the Antichrist. Of course Nero did not return from hell, nor will he ever. The Antichrist will be a man living at the time of the end who will fulfill the prophecies written about him.

Why would some early teachers and writers suggest that Nero would be the future Antichrist? Their theory was mostly based upon two passages in the Apocalypse; first, that the future beast would have a deadly wound to one of its heads, but would live to the amazement of the world (see Revelation 13:3). Nero, a great persecutor of Christians, committed suicide, thus a deadly wound. Some suggested he would rise from the abyss as the Antichrist. John described the beast that "was, is not, and yet is" (Rev. 17:8, 11), and that this beast shall "ascend out of the bottomless pit" (Rev. 17:8). This was written about AD 95, around twenty-seven years after Nero's death. Some suggested Nero was this beast who was (he existed in the past), is not (he is dead), and shall ascend (will come back from the dead).

The deadly wound in Revelation 13:3, however, is not to a man's head (singular). The wound is to one of the seven heads of the beast, referring to the death blow of one of the seven empires of Bible prophecy. After years of study, I believe this is Babylon.

The beast arising out of the abyss is interesting, as *abyss* is the Greek word translated as "bottomless pit" (Rev. 9:1, 2, 11; 11:7; 20:1, 3). This deep, underground chamber located within the Earth is where countless fallen angels are now bound in chains, awaiting a heavenly judgment (2 Pet. 2:4; Jude 6). A powerful fallen angel who oversees the abyss is a king who is called *Abaddon* in Hebrew and *Apollyon* in Greek; both names translate as *destruction*, or *destroyer* (Rev. 9:11).

When John wrote of the beast that was, is not, and yet is, he was not referring to a dead emperor, but to a fallen spirit that once influenced major empires. This spirit is now concealed in the abyss and will be loosed in the Tribulation. This destructive, beast-like spirit will empower the Antichrist to unite his ten kings and assist in forming an eighth and final earthly kingdom (see Rev. 17:11). John revealed that this beast will arise from the abyss and go into perdition (Rev. 17:11). The Greek word for "perdition" is *apoleia*, which refers to loss, ruin and destruction. During the Tribulation, numerous spirits are released from the abyss onto the earth, where they torment people (see Revelation 9). This includes four angels now bound under the river Euphrates (Rev. 9:14).

Referring to the Nero tradition, the previously noted apocalyptic passages have nothing to do with Nero being removed from his eternal confinement in hell, and then being released back on Earth to assault the Jewish people and bring persecution in a time of global judgment. This would require that Nero be raised from the dead, possess a resurrected body in some form, and be slain again, since the Antichrist will be destroyed with the brightness of Christ's coming (see 2 Thessalonians 2:8).

At times, it is possible to view prophetic scriptures from an incorrect perspective. One such example is when Christ predicted there would be some among His disciples who would not taste death until they see the Son of Man coming in His kingdom (Matt. 16:28). After Christ's resurrection, He predicted that Peter would live to be an old man and be led where he didn't want to go (John 21:18). In verse 21, Peter turned to John and asked Christ, "What shall this man do?" Jesus answered Peter, "If I will that he remain till I come, what is that to you?"

John wrote an interesting follow up to this comment:

> "Then this saying went out among the brethren that this disciple would not die. Yet, Jesus did not say to him that he would not die, but, 'If I will that he remains till I come, what is that to you?' "
>
> – JOHN 21:23 (NKJV)

When Christ predicted that someone among His disciples would not die until he saw the Son of Man coming in the kingdom, many disciples believed John would be living when Christ returned. We know John outlived all other original disciples and died around AD

100. Prior to his death, John did live to *see the kingdom* (Matt. 16:28) in a vision while exiled on the island of Patmos. John saw events, transitions, and heavenly realities that no other biblical writer saw. When John died, Christ had not returned for the church as many had anticipated.

In fact, severe persecution by different Roman Emperors broke out against Christians. First, Nero beheaded Paul and Peter. A second wave of persecution came with Diocletian, who boiled John in oil. Miraculously, John survived, forcing Diocletian to banish John to Patmos, a small, desolate, rocky island surrounded by the Aegean Sea. As the persecution against Christians continued after John's death, believers were disappointed that Christ had not returned as many had expected. Circumstances gave rise to the theory that the Imperial Roman Empire was the beast system, and an Emperor would arise as the Antichrist and persecute the saints. This school of thought prevailed during ten major persecutions of Christians that lasted over hundreds of years, until the rise of the Emperor Constantine (AD 306 to 337), who issued an edict that protected Christianity.

By the fifth century, the apocalyptic and prophetic theology of Christ's return was once again altered to accommodate the times. With the collapse of the Western Roman Empire and the rise of Christianity, Rome became the headquarters for Western Christianity and Byzantium the branch for Eastern Christianity. When this occurred, a different interpretation of prophetic events emerged. It was taught that the church was the kingdom and the popes were the vicars of Christ, under divine mandate to set up Christ's kingdom upon the earth. This led to "replacement theology," in which bishops taught that Christians were the "true Israel of God," and that God's covenant with the Jews was void. From the fifth century onward, the emphasis was upon the Roman and Byzantine Church, and their assignments to rule and reign with Christ through the church.

Any teaching of the rapture or a catching away was not on their spiritual viewfinder for many centuries. It would be the 1800s before gifted writers would release prophetic books that predicted the fall of the Turkish Empire that ruled from Palestine; the rise of Britain and

America; and the eventual return of the Jews to retake the land that the Romans had named Palestine.

Rapture critics have written me letters in which they say that the rapture is a modern teaching from the 1800s, thus it is not a doctrine in the Bible. If we consider the end time prophecies from the Old Testament, we read where Israel will be born in a day (Isa. 66:8); the Jews will return from all the Gentile nations back to Israel (Jer. 16:14-16); Jerusalem will expand and be built up (Psa. 102:16); the desert will blossom like a rose (Isa. 35:1); Israel will fill the world with fruit (Isa. 27:6); and Israel will be surrounded by enemies, yet have a great army that will defeat them (Ezekiel 37:10 and 38:15-23). None of these prophecies could be fulfilled without the one key element that made them possible: Israel had to become a Jewish nation again.

Perhaps the rapture teaching was not emphasized, not because the catching away of the church cannot be found in the Bible, but because in previous generations, there was no fulfillment of the specific signs of the Messiah's return. Also, there were prophetic verses that made no sense to previous generations. How could every eye see Christ as He returns (Rev. 1:7)? Or how could every person receive a mark in their forehead or right hand that gives the ability to buy and sell (Rev. 13:17-18)? How could a major city that rules over the kings of the earth be destroyed in just one hour (Rev. 18:3-19)? There was no possible way for any of those prophecies to be fulfilled in the time of the early church. However, our generation understands how all of these things are possible. With global satellite technology, Christ can be in one location, and every eye can see Him. With chips, invisible tattoos, and massive computers, each person can now receive a mark to buy and sell goods. Nuclear weapons can destroy an entire city in one hour—something that would have been impossible in John's day.

After much study and research, I believe that one reason bishops and ministers in the church did not emphasize the return of Christ until the 1800s was because there were no specific, prophetic signs being fulfilled that pointed to His return. British and English ministers were some of the first to decipher biblical timeframes and predict possible dates marking the time of the end. Others, such as Professor

S.W. Watson, wrote a noted prophetic thesis in which he stated that Israel would be restored as a nation, Jerusalem would become the capital of Israel, and the Jews would return from the Gentile nations—all as signs of the return of Christ.

For the early fathers not to emphasize Christ's return for the church, but to emphasize Daniel's and John's end-time beast kingdom and the Tribulation, can be blamed on the persecution of their day. They believed their circumstances indicated that certain prophecies were on the verge of fulfillment. For centuries to pass without ministers preaching the soon return of Christ is not troubling.

Also, as the eastern and western churches implemented man-made forms and rituals, they forsook numerous New Testament doctrines. Hundreds of years would pass and God would raise up people to restore lost truth. Such was the case with Martin Luther, who saw a revelation on justification by faith. Years later the Wesley brothers revived the teaching of sanctification following justification. The nineteenth century became a significant period when prophetic teaching was restored, as wars, the rise of Zionism, and the outpouring of the Holy Spirit triggered a new interest in Bible prophecy.

Following the horrible holocaust that violently took the lives of six million innocent Jews, including a million and a half children, there was a groundswell of support for the land now known as Israel. Many of the world's nations, led by the United States and Russia, were moved with compassion toward the Jewish survivors of the Nazi concentration camps and voted to implement the Partition Plan to divide the land and allow the Jews to carve out a nation in the same land God had promised Abraham. From the pivotal date of May 14, 1948, when the British mandate ended at midnight and Israel was proclaimed a new nation, Bibles that had sat on shelves were dusted off. Ministers and teachers began to pore over possible clues to discover what would follow next and the message of the coming of the Lord was raised from obscurity.

The primary reason the prophetic message is appreciated by our generation is because the world can now see how the strange predictions of ancient prophets are aligning and coming to pass. Daniel was told to seal his book until the time of the end, when "many shall run to and fro and knowledge shall increase" (Dan. 12:4). This increase in knowledge also alludes to spiritual understanding of prophetic mysteries, as penned in Daniel and Revelation. I believe this is why, in our time, there is greater understanding on the rapture teaching and the return of Christ.

CHAPTER 13

DECODING THE YOM KIPPUR CIPHER

T HE ONE PERSON who has heard me preach more messages than any other living human is my darling wife, Pam. While discussing the prophetic meaning of the Jewish festivals, she asked me an interesting question, which I want to explain in this chapter.

I was emphasizing to her the significance of prophetic teachers and Bible students understanding the divine order of the seven festivals and how the final three—Trumpets, Atonement, and Tabernacles—have a future prophetic fulfillment. She commented, "The Day of Atonement, in my opinion, has already been fulfilled with Christ's crucifixion, since His death atoned for our sins. If so, then the only two festivals remaining to be fulfilled are Trumpets and Tabernacles; one representing the return of Christ and the other representing Christ setting up His Kingdom on Earth. Don't people who believe in a post-Tribulation rapture have a point, since they teach that the return of Christ and His reign on Earth happen during the same timeframe?"

I could understand her reasoning. In ancient Israel on the Day of Atonement, there were two goats. One was marked for the Lord and the other as the scapegoat. Three eighteen-inch red threads were used during the sacrificial ritual. At the Passover of Christ's crucifixion, Christ was the sacrifice for the Lord, while a murderer named Barabbas was the scapegoat who was released from his death sentence.

The goat for the Lord bore the sins of the people and was sacrificed on the altar. The scapegoat also bore sins, but was released into the wilderness where, in later history, it would be pushed off a mountain in the wilderness where it would meet its death. Barabbas was released as a sinner; if he remained a sinner, he died in his sins.

The three red threads were used as markers; one was tied around the neck of the goat for the Lord, and one between the horns of the scapegoat. The third was nailed to the outer temple doors, and it supernaturally turned white once the scapegoat met its death in the wilderness. Once the thread turned white, this indicated that the Israelites' sins had been forgiven and would no longer be remembered (see Isa. 1:18). Paul wrote to the Romans, "...We also joy in God through our Lord Jesus Christ, by whom we have now received the atonement" (Rom. 5:11). I teach that the *complete fulfillment* of the Day of Atonement happens when the judgments of the Great Tribulation are unleashed on Earth, as atonement is *positive for those who repent* and *negative for those who rebel and resist God's call to repentance.*

To answer this seeming contradiction of the Day of Atonement being completely fulfilled through Christ's sufferings, we must take a closer look at this sixth convocation through the eyes of God, who revealed it to Moses.

> "And the LORD spoke to Moses, saying: Also the tenth day of this seventh month shall be the Day of Atonement. It shall be a holy convocation for you; you shall afflict your souls, and offer an offering made by fire to the LORD. And you shall do no work on that same day, for it is the Day of Atonement, to make atonement for you before the LORD your God."
>
> – LEVITICUS 23:26-28 (NKJV)

The Day of Atonement is a festival that conceals an apparent contradiction within its rituals and traditions. This was a day when various animal sacrifices were offered to atone for the sins of the High Priest, the Levites, and the people of Israel. It is also an appointed day of fasting and afflicting the soul. This affliction referred to humility and submission to God through self-discipline. At the same time, the great Jubilee cycles, which occurred every fifty years, began on the Day of Atonement.

Why would this one festival encode both judgment and Jubilees—punishment and release? When we understand the dual purpose for this festival, then we can see how Christ enacted a *partial* fulfillment at this first coming and will fulfill a second phase prior to His return.

THE ASPECT OF JUDGMENT

The Torah's *moral laws* were revealed for each individual Jew, in covenant with God, to follow for their spiritual benefit and the benefit of the community as a whole. The *judicial instructions* were intended to keep the people in line with God's divine legal system for dealing with matters pertaining to property, animals, and personal and business ethics. The *sacrificial code*, including the New Moons, Sabbaths and Festivals, revealed God's system of repentance, forgiveness, and restoration for both the individual and the nation. Sacrifice included daily offerings, trespass and transgression offerings, and fellowship and thanksgiving offerings brought to the tabernacle and later the temple in Jerusalem, and intended to draw a *person* closer to God. However, the Day of Atonement was a time of *national* soul searching, humility, brokenness before God, and repentance.

The great fear that gripped the people on the Day of Atonement was evident in the yearly ritual of the concealment of the high priest. Immediately following the conclusion of the Festival of Trumpets, the high priest would conceal himself for seven days in a special chamber within the temple compound. He did this for self-evaluation and to meditate on the law and mentally review, over and over again, the rituals required for this important day. He must have no spiritual impurities or mental temptation disrupting him. Rabbinical thought expresses the three spiritual conditions of the multitude in attendance on this day as the totally righteous, the unrighteous, and others who were neither righteous nor unrighteous, but living somewhere in between.

God instructed that on this one day, the people were to afflict (chasten) their souls. The high priest would transfer sin from the people to the various animals—a bull for the high priest and his family; a ram for the Levites and their families; and goats for the general population of Israelites. There is no record in biblical history that God did not forgive His people when they turned to Him for repentance on this day. However, the day was filled with great reverence and awe, and the instruction was to seek God in repentance or encounter God's judgment for your sins.

THE DOUBLE FULFILLMENT

The Day of Atonement is a double fulfillment festival. It was partially fulfilled at Christ's first appearance and will be completely fulfilled prior to and at the return of Christ to set up His Kingdom. The best way to describe this duel fulfillment is by understanding the dual nature of the Messiah—that of the *Lamb* and the *Lion*. Christ's suffering during a Passover season was symbolized in the prophecy of Isaiah 53 as a lamb going to the slaughter (Isa. 53:7). Christ was introduced by John the baptizer as the Lamb of God who takes away the sin of the world (John 1:29). Christ was crucified on Passover, the same day thousands of lambs were being slaughtered at the temple to commemorate Israel's original redemption from Egypt. As the redemptive Lamb, Christ brought judgment to man's sins and, through His sacrifice, provided atonement and justification for sins of individuals.

At Christ's return, He will be identified as the Lion of the tribe of Judah (Rev. 5:5) and be marked as the King of Kings and Lord of Lords (Rev. 19:16). Kings oversee armies (see Rev. 19:14), conquer enemies (see Rev. 19:19-21), and rule from nations and empires (see Rev. 20:4). Christ, the Lion of Judah, will return to judge the nations and to set up His Kingdom on a Day of Atonement. On this day, Satan is judged (Rev. 20:3) and Israel is redeemed (Isa. 51:11).

As it relates to the Day of Atonement, the principle of the past and future fulfillment is evident when we review a passage found in Isaiah. The verse is a dynamic Messianic prophecy, written hundreds of years before Christ quoted the passage while in Nazareth. Isaiah wrote:

> "The Spirit of the Lord GOD is upon me; because the LORD hath anointed me to preach good tidings unto the meek; he hath sent

me to bind up the brokenhearted, to proclaim liberty to the captives, and the opening of the prison to them that are bound; To
proclaim the acceptable year of the LORD, and the day of vengeance of our God; to comfort all that mourn."

–ISAIAH 61:1-2 (KJV)

After forty days of fasting, Christ returned to Nazareth on the
Sabbath day and entered the synagogue, where He was presented the
scroll of Isaiah. He found this Isaiah passage and stood before His
hometown crowd to announce:

"The Spirit of the Lord is upon me, because he hath anointed
me to preach the gospel to the poor, he hath sent me to heal the
brokenhearted, to preach deliverance to the captives, the recovery
of sight to the blind, to set at liberty them that are bruised, to
preach the acceptable year of the Lord."

– LUKE 4:18-19

Notice that Christ did not quote all of Isaiah's prediction. He
omitted, "and the day of vengeance of our God; to comfort all that
mourn." He did, however, declare to those listening that the acceptable year of the Lord had come. The reason Christ spoke of the acceptable year of the Lord and refrained from saying He came to proclaim
the day of vengeance, is because the day of vengeance is the future
Great Tribulation in which God's wrath is poured out on the nations.

Christ appeared during His earthly ministry as the Lamb and not
the Lion. The phrase "acceptable year of the Lord" is a reference to
the year of Jubilee, a set time that reoccurred every forty-nine years.
On the fiftieth year, the silver trumpet was blasted on the tenth day
of the seventh month, which was the Day of Atonement. On the fif-
ty-year Jubilee, every Jewish slave was given their freedom and had to
be released from their slave masters. Also, any land that previously had
been sold could be redeemed back to the original owner. The Jubilee
was a year of release, liberty, and freedom on both an individual and
national level.

Christ was confirming that He was the fulfillment of Isaiah's
prophecy. In Greek, the word "acceptable" is *dektos* and refers to the

people mentioned in the prophecy who previously were unable to receive much-needed ministry. Through Christ the spiritual captives are released, the poor receive the Gospel, and the broken-hearted are mended. Thus the Jubilee was no longer a set year, but was now Christ Himself! Christ's Jubilee message was one of liberty, freedom, and release—from sin, sickness, demonic influence, and spiritual captivity. As the Redeeming Lamb, Christ came to destroy the works of the devil (1 John 3:8) and set men free (John 8:36). There was no vengeance or wrath in Christ's message or ministry. It was simply a message of liberty and freedom.

The secular Jewish New Year begins during the Festival of Trumpets. The Jubilee year is proclaimed nine days later with trumpet blasts on the Day of Atonement. Every seven years is a sabbatical cycle (called a Shemitah), and every seventh Shemitah introduces a Jubilee, which begins at the end of the forty-ninth year and continues through the fiftieth year. It seems the announcement of the Jubilee year should come on the New Year—on Trumpets and not on Atonement. Why was Jubilee proclaimed with a silver trumpet on Atonement? The answer is found in the dual nature of Atonement—judgment and release—and specifically that Messiah would become mankind's Jubilee through redemption and forgiveness through His blood.

As the Lamb, the Jubilee announcement fulfills part of the atonement pattern though Christ's sufferings. The future fulfillment will be unveiled at the return of the King, the Lion of Judah. This will also complete the second part of the Isaiah prophecy, "...and the day of vengeance of our God...." The word vengeance is found twenty-eight times in thirty-two verses in the Old Testament. It means "to revenge and to avenge; to pay back for evil." The first biblical reference is found when God warned of His vengeance if anyone slew Cain in retaliation for murdering his brother (Gen. 4:15). The second reference to vengeance is found in God's warning to Moses:

> "For their vine is of the vine of Sodom and of the fields of Gomorrah; their grapes are grapes of gall, their clusters are bitter. Their wine is the poison of serpents, and the cruel venom of cobras.

Is this not laid up in store with Me, sealed up among My trea-sures? Vengeance is Mine, and recompense; their foot shall slip in due time; for the day of their calamity is at hand, and the things to come hasten upon them."

– Deut. 32:32-35 (NKJV)

Notice the phrases found here that we will see repeated in the book of Revelation concerning the future Great Tribulation:

- Vine of Sodom

- Grapes of gall

- Bitter clusters

- Vengeance

A reflection of the warning in Deuteronomy is penned in John's apocalyptic vision in Revelation:

"And another angel came out from the altar, which had power over fire; and cried with a loud cry to him that had the sharp sickle, saying, Thrust in thy sharp sickle, and gather the clusters of the vine of the earth; for her grapes are fully ripe. And the angel thrust in his sickle into the earth, and gathered the vine of the earth, and cast it into the great winepress of the wrath of God. And the winepress was trodden without the city, and blood came out of the winepress, even unto the horse bridles, by the space of a thousand and six hundred furlongs."

– Rev. 14:18-20 (KJV)

The vine of Sodom (Duet. 32:32) is a metaphor which indicates that the same spiritual fruit (abominations) the inhabitants of Sodom pro-duced will grow again in the time of the end. In Revelation 11, the iniquities of Jerusalem are compared spiritually to Sodom (Rev. 11:8). John's description of God's wrath being released is that of a vine where grapes are harvested and crushed. John's "grapes of wrath" metaphor is connected to Moses' statement of "grapes of gall." Moses spoke of the wine produced from bitter clusters, just as John described the wine-press of God's wrath being poured out on the world. The imagery painted by John is that of God harvesting the ripened grapes from the world's vine and crushing them in His winepress. Instead of the red blood of grapes, human blood pours from the winepress, indicating massive deaths from apocalyptic wars and violence.

Moses alluded to God's vengeance and connected it to the iniquity of Sodom and Gomorrah. In 2 Thessalonians 1:8, Paul spoke of Christ's return at the conclusion of the future Tribulation and described Christ in this manner: in flaming fire taking vengeance on those who do not know God, and on those who do not obey the gospel of our Lord Jesus Christ.

Moses first penned the revelation of God's vengeance and gave a detailed description of the destruction of human flesh:

> "If I whet My glittering sword, and My hand takes hold on judgment, I will render vengeance to My enemies, and repay those who hate Me. I will make My arrows drunk with blood, and My sword shall devour flesh, with the blood of the slain and the captives, from the heads of the leaders of the enemy. Rejoice, O Gentiles, with his people; for He will avenge the blood of His servants, and render vengeance to His adversaries; He will provide atonement for His land and His people."
>
> – DEUT. 32:41-43 (NKJV)

This detailed imagery can be compared with Paul's 2 Thessalonians prophecy of Christ defeating the Antichrist armies and taking vengeance on his enemies. In Hebrew, *baraq* is the word for the phrase "glittering sword." It comes from the root word meaning "lightning." Christ's sudden return to Earth is compared to lightning shining from the east to the west (Matt. 24:27). When Christ returns with the holy angels and the armies of heaven, His words are as a sharp two-edged sword coming from His mouth and devouring His enemies (Rev. 1:16; 19:15, 21). Thus Christ is judging with His sword, just as Moses indicated the Lord would do.

One of the amazing Messianic prophecies that gives great detail about Christ's return and defeat of the armies of the Antichrist is found in Isaiah 63:1-6:

"Who is this that cometh from Edom, with dyed garments from Bozrah? this that is glorious in his apparel, travelling in the greatness of his strength? I that speak in righteousness, mighty to save. Wherefore art thou red in thine apparel, and thy garments like him that treadeth in the winefat? I have trodden the winepress alone; and of the people there was none with me: for I will tread them in mine anger, and trample them in my fury; and their blood shall be sprinkled upon my garments, and I will stain all my raiment.

For the day of vengeance is in mine heart, and the year of my redeemed is come. And I looked, and there was none to help; and I wondered that there was none to uphold: therefore mine own arm brought salvation unto me; and my fury, it upheld me. And I will tread down the people in mine anger, and make them drunk in my fury, and I will bring down their strength to the earth."

– Isa. 63:1-6 (KJV)

There are parallels between this prophecy, Moses' insights in Deuteronomy, and John's vision in the Apocalypse. Isaiah is speaking of the Messiah, who has tread the winepress and whose garments are red with blood. The winepress imagery is repeated in Revelation 14:19. John saw Christ's garments dipped in blood when He returned to Earth at the conclusion of the Tribulation (Rev. 19:13). From Isaiah's prophetic view, the Messiah is alone when battling His enemies, which indicated Christ will take on the armies of the world by Himself, and defeat them with the brightness of His coming (2 Thess. 2:8) and the sword of His mouth (Rev. 19:21). Notice Isaiah alludes to two phrases: "the day of vengeance" and "the year of my redeemed".

The day of vengeance is a term also identified as the "Day of the Lord" in numerous passages (Isa. 13:6, 9; 34:8; Jer. 46:10). Christ's return to Earth will be the climax of the Great Tribulation. This Day of the Lord will initiate the "year of my redeemed." This phrase is linked to the Jubilee, or the "the acceptable year of the Lord" (Luke 4:19). Christ will be returning with the armies of heaven (see Rev. 19) to destroy His enemies on the Day of Atonement (note Deut. 32:43). Yet on the same Day of Atonement, Christ will immediately set in motion the liberation and redemption of His Jewish elect (see Matt. 24:31).

The Day of Atonement was designed to be a *release from sin*, and when sins were forgiven, blessings were released upon all of Israel during the next festival, the Feast of Tabernacles, which occurred five days following the Day of Atonement. The seven days of Tabernacles are called by devout Jews the "seasons of joy," as joy is always the spiritual benefit released following repentance. Peter confirmed this when he spoke to his Jewish audience on the Day of Pentecost and reminded them that if they repented, the times of refreshing would come from the presence of the Lord (Acts 3:19).

On the last day of the seven-year Tribulation, God's wrath and the final judgments peak on Earth and the unrepentant are destroyed at the return of the Messiah and His armies. The remnant of Jews scattered abroad among the nations will be gathered back to the land with the sound of angelic trumpets, as angels are assigned to the four points of Earth to bring the Lord's redeemed back to Zion. Christ spoke of this when He said that, after the Tribulation, He will send His angels with the sound of a trumpet to gather His elect from the four regions: north, south, east, and west (Matt. 24:31). Two prophetic passages from Isaiah underscore the Messiah's plan to gather His redeemed:

> "And it shall come to pass in that day, that the great trumpet shall be blown, and they shall come which were ready to perish in the land of Assyria, and the outcasts in the land of Egypt, and shall worship the LORD in the holy mount at Jerusalem."
>
> – Isaiah 27:13 (KJV)

> "Therefore the redeemed of the Lord shall return, and come with singing unto Zion; and everlasting joy shall be upon their head: they shall obtain gladness and joy; and sorrow and mourning shall flee away."
>
> – Isaiah 51:11 (KJV)

Satan's Confinement

The Apocalypse explains the order of events once Christ returns with the armies of heaven, captures the beast and the false prophet, and confines them in the lake of fire. In John's vision, following the dethronement of the Antichrist and his system, Satan becomes the next target of the Messiah. On the very day Christ returns, He expels Satan from Earth and confines him in the bottomless pit, known in the Greek as the abyss (Rev. 20:2-3). Since Christ's final judgment against the sinner and the release of His redeemed falls at the time of Atonement, how does this fit the scenario of Satan's confinement?

A belief among rabbis and devout Jews may link Atonement and Satan's binding. The revelation of all seven festivals, including Atonement, was given to Moses in the wilderness. Jews knew there was a fallen angel named Satan who was working on Earth against God's plans. A Jewish tradition emerged that, on the Day of Atonement, God limits Satan's access and influence to accuse Israel. Thus, in the temple days, God literally forbade Satan from entering any part of the temple compound where the Atonement rituals were being performed by the High Priest.

Using the Hebrew alphabet and the numerical equivalent of each letter, the phrase "the Satan" is transliterated into the original Hebrew with four letters—hei, shin, tet and nun:

Hebrew Letter	Numerical Equivalent
H (hei)	5
S (shin)	300
T (tet)	9
N (nun)	50
	364

There are 365.25 days in a solar year, and the total of "the Satan" is 364. The difference is one day. From this a tradition emerged that there is one day when God forbids Satan to use his power as an accuser against Israel and that is on the Day of Atonement.

Rabbis note that according to Leviticus 16:10, there is a scapegoat that symbolically carries all of the sins of Israel into the Judean wilderness, and removes them from the temple and God's presence. Selected priests would lead the goat to the top of the Mount of the Azazel and push the goat off the mountain where it fell to its death hundreds of feet in the valley below, so that it could not bring sin back into the land. This was the imagery of God permanently removing the sins of Israel, giving them a clean slate, and erasing the possible judgment set against them.

In Revelation 12, the warring archangel Michael, the chief angel who deals directly with Satan, hurls Satan and his angels out of the second heaven and casts them down to the earth. A voice is then heard instructing all of heaven to rejoice since the accuser is now cast out of heaven and can no longer accuse the saints.

The timing of Satan's expulsion from the cosmic realm, where he has accused men and women before God day and night (Rev. 12:10), happens about the same time the heavenly judgment of the righteous occurs (Rev. 11:18). Since this is a heavenly tribunal, a judgment to see who is worthy to be rewarded and who is not, Satan's influence is banned and his expulsion provides him no voice against anyone standing before God at the bema judgment. This is likely one reason for his removal from his position as an accuser. Those in heaven will be rejoicing, as no charges from Satan can be leveled against them. However, those on Earth will be in great danger, as Satan will be coming down and releasing great wrath on the Earth's inhabitants (see Rev. 12:12).

A DAY TO SEAL THINGS

Today among devout Jews, there is a time known as the forty days of Teshuvah. This season begins the first of Elul and concludes forty days later on the Day of Atonement. This is their set time for individual and national repentance. If a person truly turns to God and seeks forgiveness and His righteousness, then God seals a decision on the Day of Atonement in their favor, and plans blessings for the following twelve months. God's verdict is sealed on the Day of Atonement.

This concept of sealing corresponds with the prophetic imagery described by John in Revelation 20:3. When Satan is bound and thrust into a bottomless pit under the earth, we read where the angel "sets a seal upon him." We do not know what this seal is, but we know that it prevents Satan from being released from his underground prison for a thousand years (Rev. 20:3).

MOSES' PICTURE OF THE SECOND COMING

When Moses brought Israel out of over four hundred years of Egyptian influence and captivity, Moses met God on Mount Sinai on two different occasions, each for forty days. Moses went up and the Lord came down—two times, not just once.

The first ascent was in Exodus 19, when the voice of a trumpet waxed loud and long, and the Lord came down and Moses went up (Exod. 19:20). Between the first and second ascent, there was a major disruption as Moses came down, saw Israel in idolatry, and broke the set of Commandments. Moses ascended the second time for another forty days, and the Lord came down again and gave Moses the second set of Commandments. When Moses came off the mount and was seen by the people, his face was radiating the glory of the Lord and a veil was placed over his face.

These two narratives have distinct prophetic parallels. The first parallel is there were two sets of commandments—one which was *broken* and a second which *replaced* the first and was preserved in the Ark of the Covenant (Heb. 9:4). I see this as the imagery of the first and second covenants. The first covenant was given to Israel and they were unable to keep God's laws and instructions; thus they broke the Commandments. However, God gave a New Covenant through Christ that is now being kept by believers around the world as they hide God's Word in their hearts.

Notice during the first forty days, there was no glory or veil on Moses' face. However, when he descended off the mountain the second time with the new set of stones, he manifested visible glory from God. However, Israel could not see Moses' face, as he veiled it from the people. In this imagery I see the New Covenant that replaced the first. The New Covenant is a covenant of glory revealed through Christ's crucifixion and resurrection. The Bible teaches that the eyes of the natural Jews are veiled from understanding, or seeing the glory of the covenant of Christ the Messiah. Paul addressed this:

> "Therefore, since we have such hope, we use great boldness of speech —unlike Moses, who put a veil over his face so that the children of Israel could not look steadily at the end of what was passing away. But their minds were blinded. For until this day the same veil remains unlifted in the reading of the Old Testament, because the veil is taken away in Christ. But even to this day, when Moses is read, a veil lies on their heart. Nevertheless when one turns to the Lord, the veil is taken away. Now the Lord is the Spirit; and where the Spirit of the Lord is, there is liberty. But we all, with unveiled face, beholding as in a mirror the glory of the Lord, are being transformed into the same image from glory to glory, just as by the Spirit of the Lord."
>
> – 2 CORINTHIANS 3:12-18 (NKJV)

Moses' veil concealed God's glory from the eyes of ancient Israel. The old was passing away and the new was coming forth. Paul said those in his day were spiritually blind and could not see the glory in Christ. However, when they believe, the veil is removed and they receive liberty!

There is another interesting parallel between Moses' first and second ascent. The first ascent paints the imagery of the rapture of the church, while the second ascent is a picture of the return of Christ to Earth in which His glory will be revealed. During the first ascent the people became careless, drunken, and inattentive, which is the warning Christ gave concerning His return. He said that men should watch and pray, as some will become careless and drunk prior to His return (Luke 12:45). The Israelites became careless as Moses delayed coming down from the mount. When Moses did return to the camp, three-thousand people were slain for idolatry.

When Moses returned forty days after the second ascent, two important statements must be noted. First, the Lord "descended in a cloud" and announced He would "drive out the enemy" (Exod. 34:5-11). When Christ returns in clouds of glory, He will destroy His enemies and drive the enemies of Israel from their covenant land. This will be at the second coming of Christ, and the Jewish remnant and Tribulation survivors will see the glory of God through Christ the Messiah of the world.

Moses received the Law from God during Pentecost. However, when he walked off the mount the second time, covered in the glory of God, it was on the Day of Atonement, just as Christ's second descent will be on the Day of Atonement. We can also compare Moses' two ascents on the mountain to Christ descending to save the church (1 Thess. 4:16-17). The second time He descends to save Israel:

> "The LORD will save the tents of Judah first, so that the glory of the house of David and the glory of the inhabitants of Jerusalem shall not become greater than that of Judah. In that day the LORD will defend the inhabitants of Jerusalem; the one who is feeble among them in that day shall be like David, and the house of David shall be like God, like the Angel of the LORD before them. It shall be in that day I will seek to destroy all the nations that come against Jerusalem. And I will pour on the house of David and on the inhabitants of Jerusalem the Spirit of grace and supplication; then they will look on me whom they pierced. Yes, they will mourn for Him as one mourns for his only son, and grieve for Him as one grieves for a firstborn.
>
> – ZECH. 12:7-10 (NKJV)

The seven years (Daniel's seventieth week - Daniel 9) will be a time of Jacob's (Israel's) trouble. Zechariah noted that two-thirds of the land's inhabitants will be cut off, while one-third will survive and remain in the land (Zech. 13:8). Zechariah predicted that the third would come through the fire and would call upon the name of the Lord (Zech. 13:9). Christ will defend Judah and Jerusalem, destroy enemy nations, and intervene in the battle of Armageddon (Rev. 16:16). He will liberate His people from the iron dominion of the Antichrist.

When Christ returns, those on Earth will question Him about His wounds, or the scars from His piercings (Zech. 13:6). The scars in Christ's hands will remind all on Earth of His death and redemptive plan that was previewed in the ancient Atonement rituals. The crown on His head will remind them that He is the King and the Jubilee.

Thus, the Day of Atonement has two applications. The release from sin and redemption was completed at the cross of Christ. However, the Jubilee that frees the land and returns it to its original owners (the Jews) will have its fulfillment when Christ the King sets up His throne in Jerusalem for one thousand years! This will be a continuous Jubilee, and each year the Festival of Tabernacles will be celebrated in Jerusalem to commemorate the Messiah's Kingdom.

> "And it shall come to pass that everyone who is left of all the nations which came against Jerusalem shall go up from year to year to worship the King, the LORD of hosts, and to keep the Feast of Tabernacles. And it shall be that whichever of the families of the earth do not come up to Jerusalem to worship the King, the LORD of hosts, on them there will be no rain. If the family of Egypt will not come up and enter in, they shall have no rain; they shall receive the plague with which the LORD strikes the nations who do not come up to keep the Feast of Tabernacles. This shall be the punishment of Egypt and the punishment of all the nations that do not come up to keep the Feast of Tabernacles."
>
> – ZECHARIAH 14:16-19 (NKJV)

Five days after the Day of Atonement begins the Feast of Tabernacles, also known as the "seasons of our joy." This feast is a reminder of Israel's forty years of wandering in the wilderness. However, the primary theme is God's supernatural provision, when He gave them manna (angel's food) and water from a rock (see Psa. 78:24-29). Their shoes and clothes never wore out.

During the eight days in which they live outside their homes under handmade booths, the Jews are reminded to be separated from the world and from worldly desires, and to place their complete trust in God. During the millennial reign of Christ, each year the nations will "go up to the mountain of the Lord, to the house of the God of Jacob" (Isa. 2:3).

The coming of Christ to take the believers to heaven (Trumpets) will be followed by the Great Tribulation (Atonement) which will end with the return of Christ to the earth to place a seal upon Satan, and to defeat the Antichrist and all enemies of unrighteousness. This will be followed by the seasons of joy, with the saints and the survivors of the Tribulation rejoicing in their King and Messiah and enjoying their day of freedom!

CLOSING COMMENTS

Since the age of sixteen, in all my time of study, research, and documentation of biblical truths, I've found two studies are particularly riveting. One is the prophetic parallels between the days of Lot and Noah, and the days prior to Christ's return. The other is the study of the mysteries of the prophetic past and future concealed in the Jewish festivals. In this book, I have attempted to open your understanding to the prophetic parallels concealed within these two topics.

While there will be those who differ with my thesis concerning the timing of the rapture as it relates to the divine order of God, they will have difficulty disproving the fact that God set these festivals in a specific order of fulfillment, and Trumpets is without a doubt next on God's prophetic cycle.

Hopefully this book has inspired you and will cause you to search further into these marvelous truths that God has concealed in the prophetic feasts and the symbolisms that He told Daniel would be understood at the time of the end (Dan. 12:4, 9).

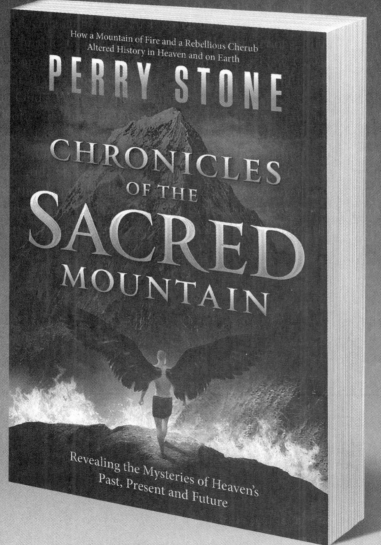

THE DEMISE OF THE AMERICAN REPUBLIC!

IS AMERICA FALLING APART?

America's Blessings are in Danger of Being Lost

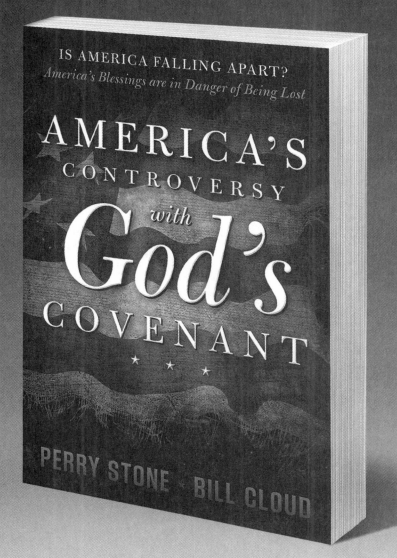